Psychic Power for Teens

Get What You Want at Home, at School, and Everywhere Else

Theresa Cheung and Terry Silvers

ADAMS MEDIA

AVON, MASSACHUSETTS

Published by Adams Media,
an F+W Publications Company
57 Littlefield Street, Avon, MA 02322. U.S.A.
www.adamsmedia.com

ISBN: 1-59337-111-X

Printed in Canada.

J I H G F E D C B A

Library of Congress Cataloging-in-Publication Data
Cheung, Theresa.
Psychic power for teens / Theresa Cheung and Terry Silvers.
p.   cm.
ISBN 1-59337-111-X
1. Teenagers--Psychic ability. I. Silvers, Terry. II. Title.
BF1045.T43C48   2005
133.8'0835--dc22   2004002407

This publication is designed to provide accurate and authoritative information with regard to the subject matter covered. It is sold with the understanding that the publisher is not engaged in rendering legal, accounting, or other professional advice. If legal advice or other expert assistance is required, the services of a competent professional person should be sought.
—From a *Declaration of Principles* jointly adopted by a Committee of the American Bar Association and a Committee of Publishers and Associations

Many of the designations used by manufacturers and sellers to distinguish their product are claimed as trademarks. Where those designations appear in this book and Adams Media was aware of a trademark claim, the designations have been printed in initial capital letters.

This book is available at quantity discounts for bulk purchases.
For information, call 1-800-872-5627.

Contents

One

Psych Yourself Out

* *Wouldn't you like to be able to sense things?*
* *Wouldn't it be great to know what your friends or teachers are really thinking?*
* *Wouldn't it be amazing if you just knew what was going to happen next?*
* *What if you could will something hard enough and make it happen?*
* *What if you could attract anyone or anything you wanted into your life?*

This book can help you do all of the above and more. The really interesting stuff, though, isn't just mind reading or divination. The really interesting stuff is finding out about *you*. Developing psychic ability can mean many things, but ultimately it is about getting to know yourself better, developing your potential, and being the best that you can be.

Five Minutes to Midnight

If the life span so far of our earth were measured as twenty-four hours, humans would not have shown up until five minutes to midnight. As incredible as it may seem, the human race is still very young. We aren't really that much different from our Stone Age ancestors. Over the centuries we have not changed very much, but the world we live in has. Our brains are still trying to catch up with the speed of change around us.

Stone Age people were naturally psychic. Think about it. If you were aware that any minute of the day you could be eaten by some hungry animal, wouldn't you become super alert and be able to sense (know psychically) when danger was near?

All of us have inborn psychic abilities just like our ancestors did. It is one of our basic senses. So why don't we use it? Let's try to explain by using an example.

If someone lived in the dark for years, his or her eyes would adjust. Over time,

Psychic Spotlight

The word *psychic* comes from *psyche,* meaning soul, the creative part of you that instinctively watches over you.

that person would actually be able to see better in the dark than in the light. It's the same with psychic ability. Once civilization and modern technology came along we got lazy and stopped sensing things around us. If you don't use something you lose it. That is why, as a teen, you are very lucky. You haven't walked the earth for as long as adults have, and so your psychic abilities haven't had a chance to get rusty yet. It may be easier for you to tap into your psychic potential than it is for adults.

You may have had a psychic experience if . . .
- You get "hunches" about people.
- You know who is calling before you pick up the phone.
- You've experienced feelings of déjà vu.

Hunches are one kind of psychic experience. They are vague feelings that are hard to explain. For example, you feel uneasy for no reason when you meet someone new. You just have a hunch that he or she can't be trusted, and months later your suspicions are confirmed. This is because a part of you (your psychic part) is always watching out for you and sensing your environment. In everyday settings this sensing instinct generally fades, but in new settings or when you meet new people it becomes much more acute. Have you ever been told "You'll get used to it" when you're in an unfamiliar place or situation? When things are new we often feel more sensitive and aware. Unfortunately, we are not told how to develop this awareness—which is a shame, because it holds the key to successful psychic development.

Now that we've established that you do have psychic ability (you just aren't aware of it yet), we can move on to the next step: How do you get in touch with it?

Illogical, Captain!

What do you think of when you think of a psychic? Some of you might envision a little white-haired lady wearing a long cape and consulting a crystal ball. Or perhaps you think of the people you've seen on television talk shows, walking through the audience and talking to different people about spirits communicating from the other side. They seem to know things that they couldn't possibly know about the audience member's life, and the audience is amazed. Sound familiar? Chances are, you're thinking "What a con! They've got to have plants working in the audience."

Congratulations! You passed the first test. Questioning what you see and looking for the truth behind appearances is essential if you are to develop your psychic ability. Only fools believe everything they are told, and we have great respect for you as readers. After all, you had the wisdom to decide to read this book! As you read, we'd like you to be like Scully in the *X Files*, or Mr. Spock in *Star Trek*, always skeptical, always questioning. And don't try to tell us that you haven't seen or heard about the *X Files* or *Star Trek*—we won't believe you.

Things you should know about your psychic power:
Psychic power is not just for a special few. You are already psychic. You just don't know it yet.
- Like any skill, psychic ability takes time and practice to learn.
- You can learn to control your psychic ability—to turn it on and off at your will—whenever you like.

People develop their psychic ability for many reasons. Some want help in finding true love. Others want to know what will appear in their exam papers. Some want to know when their friends are lying. Others want to know the future. Whatever your reason, developing your psychic skills has many benefits. Here are just a few of them:

* You will realize that you are more capable than you thought.
* You will make better choices in life.
* You will be able to develop stronger relationships and become a better judge of character.
* You will be able to avoid difficulties because you will be able to foresee possible problems before they happen.
* You will be able to keep your cool under pressure and become more creative and successful in all aspects of your life.

Ready, Get Set ... Go!

Now that we have whetted your appetite, let's get down to work. Grab a pen and paper. Find a room or space without distractions where you can read this book undisturbed.

Before you try to develop your psychic power, you have to find out what makes you tick. You need to uncover the real you. Why is this important? It's important because self-awareness, or the ability to stand apart from yourself and observe your thoughts and actions, is the first step to developing psychic power and changing your life for the better.

Psychic power is a natural part of you, and its development is a reflection of your self-awareness and attitude toward life in general. So let's begin by taking a good long look at you. What kind of a person are you? Are you the kind of person who can listen to an inner voice to know right from wrong? Are you the kind of person who can envision new possibilities? Are you the kind of person who has willpower? Let's find out.

The seven-stage quiz below is a fun test to help you become more aware of your personality. Each stage is designed to give an insight into a particular area of your life, so once you've answered the first part, just move on to the next. This isn't a test with right and wrong answers, so don't stress yourself out about taking it. Have fun with it. Self-development and psychic work is best undertaken when you feel relaxed and lighthearted. We don't want you to take anything too seriously at this stage.

Well, what are you waiting for? Prepare to enter the discovery zone.

Psychic Quiz

You may not have thought about it, but even superficial things like the clothes you wear and the image you present to others send out major signals about the kind of person you are. Don't believe us? Then try this quiz.

✳ *Part One: What's Your Fashion Sense?*

1. Regardless of the weather outside, which pair of shoes do you enjoy wearing the most?
   a. Fashionable shoes
   b. Sandals or comfortable flat shoes
   ML c. Sneakers
   d. Boots

2. What is your schoolbag style?
   a. Expensive
    b. Stylish
   c. Practical
   d. Colorful and girlie/macho

3. What do you usually wear to a party?
   ML a. Jeans and a cool top
   b. Bright and colorful clothes
   c. Comfortable pants and your favorite T-shirt
   d. Smart but stylish party clothes

4. What would your ideal date be?
   ML a. A romantic picnic for two
   b. An outdoor hiking adventure
   c. Just chatting over a cup of coffee or a meal
   d. Checking out a movie

Mostly A's: Spring

You are the kind of person who loves meeting new people, and your laid-back attitude means you make a good friend. You are honest and tell others how you feel. Bet you have been caught daydreaming in class more than once, though! That's because you are always fantasizing about your next cool adventure.

Mostly B's: Summer

You are carefree and fun-loving. Summer is your favorite time of year because you get to spend so much time with your friends. And you have so many of them. You always look on the bright side of life and don't let problems get you down. You are independent and are never afraid to say what you think.

Mostly C's or a Mix of All the Letters: Autumn

You can sometimes be hard to understand because you are often changing your mind, but deep down you are a strong person. If you feel low you know how to get yourself smiling again. It takes people a while to get to know you, but once they do, you'll be friends for life. You are organized but quite sentimental. That means your room looks tidy, but there are secret stashes of junk in your closet or under your bed.

Mostly D's: Winter

Some people would say that you are shy and you only really open up to your closest pals. Nights in with your friends are way more fun for you than a massive party. You are close to your family, and you secretly enjoy spending time with them even if they can be annoying. But you wouldn't admit it to anyone. You work hard and have a disciplined approach to life that will take you far.

Part Two: Who's in Charge of Your Life?

Would you rather take the lead or follow the crowd? Think about the following questions.

* Do you like making new friends? L - Yes (+M)
* Do your friends always ask to borrow your gear? L -,Yes M -No
* When someone upsets you do you tell them about it rather than keep it inside? M + L - No
* Have you been or do you want to be on your school's student council? L + M - No
* If your crush walks toward you, do you hide behind your locker door? L + M - Yes
* Do you like to make up your own mind about things? L + M Yes

Mostly Yes: Cool and Confident

You may not know it, but your cool and sassy style inspires your friends to follow your every move. You always manage to put your individual stamp on everything, from your latest outfits to your party plans. Having loads of confidence gives you a head start, because you are proud to stand out in the crowd. Just be careful that you don't get too full of yourself—there's a big difference between having confidence and showing off. Be careful that you're not crossing the line.

⭐ Mix of Yes and No: On Balanced Ground

You like to look good and to fit in, but you are not quite the trendsetter type. You speak your mind when you need to, but you don't really want to become the organizer of the group. You might feel a bit intimidated by some situations, but you are confident enough to know that you can handle most things.

Mostly No: Cautious Cat

You are cautious about trying new things until you are totally convinced they will be okay. Taking a back seat might seem like the safe option, but why let everyone else have all the fun? Once you realize being brave doesn't have to be embarrassing, you'll be racing to take the plunge.

Part Three: What's Your Relationship Style?

Crushes can make you act differently. With all those new emotions flying around, even the coolest guy or girl can turn into something wild. So whether you are in a relationship or have your eye on someone, let's see how the opposite sex makes you behave.

1. Someone you're really interested in has just started at your school. You:
   a. Track him (or her) down and ask him out before anyone else gets a chance.
   b. Daydream about him constantly but clam up when you get within five feet of him.
   c. Try to get to know him and see what happens.
   d. Play it cool—you're not in a rush. Besides, if he likes you, he can ask you out.

2. You're finally going out on a date, but he (or she) is half an hour late. You:
   a. March to his house and demand an explanation.
   b. Give him fifteen more minutes—he could be stuck in traffic.
   c. Call his cell to find out what's going on.
   d. Call up a couple of friends and make other plans—you've got better things to do than wait around.

3. The rumor mill is going full throttle, and the latest is that your significant other is cheating. You:

a. Wallow in your anguish for a while—you put "your song" on repeat, tear up all of the photos of you together, and burn his (or her) letters.

b. Beg him not to leave you.

c. Call and ask him what the real scoop is—no sense jumping to conclusions until you've heard the real story.

d. Ditch him. You're young and free—why waste your time on just one person?

4. You've broken up. You:

a. Tell everyone he (or she) was a loser anyway.

b. Immediately devise an action plan to win him back.

c. Are bummed for a few days, but realize it's not the end of the world.

d. Sigh with relief. Now you can do your own thing again.

5. It's your best friend's birthday and you're throwing a major party, but your love interest wants to go out with friends instead. You:

a. Sulk until he (or she) agrees to come to the party.

b. Skip the party to hang out with his friends instead—your best friend will get over it.

c. Invite him and all of his friends to the party. The more the merrier!

d. Hey, you're not attached at the hip, right? You go to the party and have a blast without him—you'll catch him tomorrow.

Mostly A's

You know exactly what you want—especially from someone you're dating. While it's good to stand your ground, you tend to overreact a bit, which can make you seem a bit scary to those around you. Try to chill out and see things from other people's points of view, or you may end up pushing away those you care about.

Mostly B's

Don't be such a doormat. You've gotta let others know what you want or you'll always get dragged along with the crowd. Relationships are about two people. If your love interest is walking all over you, maybe it's time to call it quits. The most important thing to remember is to be true to yourself.

Mostly C's

You've got this relationship thing well and truly figured out. You don't let people take advantage of you, and if there is a problem you stay calm and cool until it's sorted out. Your levelheaded attitude means that partners know exactly where they stand, and they love that.

Mostly D's

Phew! You are so lukewarm about your relationship that you don't really care if you are with someone or not. It's great that you are not dependent on someone else to make you happy, but don't take things too far or you may well end up on your own. Knowing your own mind means that when you do find someone you like they will probably be as chilled-out and laid-back as you are.

Part Four: What Kind of a Friend Are You?

It's not easy to tell what others think about you, though you may already have an idea. Well, who better to ask than your closest friends? Someone who cares about you will always be truthful with you. Ask a friend the following questions and see what you learn about yourself.

What you hear may surprise you.

1. How would they describe you in three words? Cute, Creative + Loving
2. What is your best quality? How much i care about him how
3. Why do they enjoy your company? obsessive i am and how loving i am.
. Beause i'm loving and i make him feel like i'm
safe and at home. Ant
Part Five: What's Your Ideal Job? i'm sexy.

Read the following sentences and rate them on a scale of 1 to 3.
1 means "I agree," 2 means "maybe or sometimes or not sure," and 3
means "no way."

2 I'm not the most organized person in the world. M - 1
1 I read extra books just for fun. M - 1
2 Solving problems is not my strongest skill. M - 1
1 Playing computer games is boring. M - 2
1 I daydream a lot. M - 1
1 I keep a diary and write in it all the time. M - 1
3 If someone is upsetting me, I'll tell him or her. M - 2
1 I don't enjoy math. M - 1
2 I really want to be famous. M = 1
1 Romantic films are better than action ones. M - 1
1 I'm not very good with money. M - 1
3 I hate personal organizers. M - 1

Mostly 1's

You enjoy English and history. It's great that you are so imaginative.
Make the most of it. You'd rather write stories or make up new games
than watch TV or play video games. You'd make a great actor, teacher,
journalist, or musician. Keep doing the things you really enjoy, and you'll
be a great success no matter which career you eventually choose.

Mostly 2's

You enjoy science and art, which means there is no limit to what you might do. You could be anything from a chef to a politician. You don't have to make up your mind right now, though. Try getting involved in lots of activities at school to help you discover what you enjoy the most.

Mostly 3's

You are logical and good with numbers. You enjoy organizing other people and fixing things. Being good at science is a real bonus for any job you have later in life. If you decide to be a nurse, a doctor, a vet, or a chemist, you'll be great at it.

Part Six: You

1. Which color are you most drawn to at this moment?

yellow   blue   red

green

Yellow

You are in a great mood, and now is a good time to make decisions. Write a list of all the things that have been bugging you lately and get them sorted out. Don't forget to get out there and spread your fabulous feelings among your friends.

Blue

Is there something on your mind? Whatever it is, sitting around worrying about it won't get you anywhere. So clear your head by doing something you like—take a walk, read a book, write in your journal, hang out with friends. Sometimes putting a little distance between you and the problem will bring you a solution in no time.

Green

This color signifies change, so if you've been considering something new—a new look, a new job, whatever—this could be the day to go for it. You are a major influence on your friends right now, so be careful if you are dishing out advice.

Red

You've been putting something off for weeks and it is time to tackle it. Any more delays and it just won't get done. You are full of energy and ready for action, so make the most of your mood. Choosing a bold color means that you are feeling confident and positive.

2. Now draw the first shape that pops into your head into the space below.

Look at what you have drawn, and use the decoder that follows to discover the hidden meaning. (Make sure you draw the shape *before* looking at the decoder—no cheating!)

Circles

A sign of friendliness and honesty. They show that you are strong and independent and you love a challenge. You are feeling happy and stress-free.

Squares

You've got a logical mind. Are you good at math and science? Once you've made a decision about something you stick with it. Your goals are clearly in sight.

Straight Lines

Making tricky choices is a complete piece of cake for you. You are honest and open. With no major worries in your life, your mood is calm and relaxed.

Wobbly Lines

You've got a big decision to make and you are still thinking about it. Don't panic. Just be careful not to jump into anything before you're sure about it.

Zigzags

Something has just turned your world upside-down. You are angry or worried about a recent event.

Stars

You're a creative whiz, and you always have your head in the clouds. Your colorful imagination means you'll always find a solution to the trickiest problem.

Triangles

Balanced and focused, that's you. Your friends know they can rely on you no matter what.

Hearts

You are loving and giving and sensitive to the needs of others. Just make sure you don't neglect your own.

3. Now it's time for straight talking. Answer these questions yes or no as honestly as possible.

    Y   N

    1. If you found some money on the classroom floor, would you turn it in to your teacher? ☐ ☑ *M+L*

    2. If one of your friends was talking about you behind your back, would you confront her or him? ☐ ☑ *M+L*

    3. While making change, a cashier hands you too much money. Do you tell her? ☐ ☑ *M+L*

    4. You're hanging out with your best friend and you notice that her journal is lying open on her desk. Do you read it when she leaves the room? ☑ ☐ *M+L*

    5. You and your friend have a crush on the same person. You've heard that he likes your friend and not you. Do you tell your friend? ☐ ☑ *M+L*

Mostly Yes

Okay, so you may have told a few white lies in the past, but you wouldn't tell a lie if you thought anyone's feelings would get hurt. Your honesty means you are a loyal friend, and your closest pals trust you to tell them exactly how you feel. Well done.

17

Mostly No

You can be a little sneaky at times. If you carry on this way you could end up in big trouble. The first rule of friendship is trust. If your friends catch you telling fibs to everyone around you, they will soon realize you can't keep their secrets to yourself. Next time you are tempted to tell a lie, think again. You've been warned.

Congratulations! You've reached the final stage of the quiz. But hang on a minute—your toughest challenge is about to begin. Get ready, 'cause you've gotta think about how in touch you are with your intuition right now . . .

Part Seven: How Intuitive Are You Now?

For each question, circle the number that best describes how true this is for you.

1 = never happens
2 = rarely happens
3 = sometimes happens
4 = often happens
5 = always happens

1. The phone rings and you know who is calling you.
   1 / 2 / 3 / 4 / 5

2. You sense that your boyfriend or girlfriend is going to dump you, and a few days later he or she does. 1 / 2 / 3 / 4 / 5

3. You often understand your best friend's inner feelings even though he or she is hiding them. 1 / 2 / 3 / 4 / 5

4. You are convinced that someone is standing behind you, but when you look around there is nobody there. 1 / 2 / 3 / 4 / 5

5. You go to a new place and you feel that you know it already.
1 / 2 / 3 / (4) / (5)

6. You feel that something is meant to be and are not at all surprised when it does happen. 1 / 2 / 3 / 4 / (5) m + L

Now add up your points.

Less Than 10

What a skeptic! Though you err on the safe side of things, there's part of you that wants to explore the psychic world. Otherwise you wouldn't have picked up this book, right? You don't know it yet, but if you can loosen up a bit and open your mind, your psychic abilities could amaze even you.

Less Than 20

You do sense things but are not confident enough in your own feelings and perceptions. It's time to sharpen your skills and your senses and open the door to supercool discoveries.

Less Than 25   Matt

You're already off to a great start. You have psychic abilities, though you may not have realized that's what they were. You are a little skeptical, but this is good. The ability to question and investigate is crucial for psychic work.

25 or More   Liz

There's no doubt that you are in touch with your psychic abilities. But just because you're getting certain psychic impressions doesn't mean they are all true. A good psychic always questions the world around her or him in order to know the difference between fantasy and reality. Keep working at developing your power, but don't let your imagination get the best of you.

Try a Little Test

Grab a pen and paper and a pack of playing cards. Then settle down somewhere quiet, where you won't be disturbed. You may want to do this in the evening, when you will be more relaxed. Take the face cards and jokers out of the pack and put them aside. Place the other cards face down, keeping them together as a deck. Close your eyes and breathe deeply for a few minutes until your mind is clear and focused. Then pick up the first card and hold it face down in your hand. Take a moment to decide if it is a heart, club, spade, or diamond. Really try to feel which suit the card is rather than just guessing. Go through the whole pack, one by one, and keep track of your score.

Less Than 10

Don't panic if you got less than ten right. Mystic experts believe that all human beings have psychic power. It's just that over thousands of generations we forgot how to use it. Keep practicing to see if you can unlock yours.

Between 10 and 25

Well done. That's a good score. Mystic abilities get better the more you use them, so get shuffling and start again.

25 or More

You're a psychic in the making! It looks like your psychic power is near the surface, just waiting for you to develop and nurture it. Why not try it again, and predict the numbers this time?

Congratulations! Now that you've completed the quiz, take a few moments to check in with yourself. Did the quiz surprise you? Are you satisfied with your answers? If you want to open up to your natural psychic gifts, you really need to know how you feel about yourself and what kind of life you want to lead. Think about it: If you don't know yourself, how can you make sense of any of the psychic messages that come to you?

Being a psychic is a challenging thing to live with. As you'll learn, there are many advantages to having a vision of the future and being able to see through people and situations at a glance. Keep in mind, though, that to really benefit from being psychic takes time and experience. The happier you are with yourself, the better your psychic power will be. The best psychics are those who are not afraid of loving, giving, being honest, having a good laugh, and being themselves in any situation.

And don't think that you won't ever change. You've only just scratched the surface of what you can do. One of the best things about developing psychic power (and about growing up) is that you never stop learning about yourself and discovering skills, talents, insights, and potential you never thought you had. If there were things you discovered about yourself in the quiz that you didn't feel comfortable with, there is no reason why you can't change them. In fact, developing your natural psychic abilities can help you make those changes. Later in the book we'll explain how.

You already have within you the ability to take responsibility for your life and make positive changes and choices. You and you alone hold the key to your destiny, and developing your psychic ability will help you see just how powerful you are. Just remember—your psychic power is not what makes you strong—*you* are what makes you strong.

Your Silent Power

Now that you have managed to wade through the first chapter and have really started to think and ask questions about yourself and your life, we are going to go into some deeper waters. Don't worry, we will be the life jacket you can hold on to, and there will be lots of exercises and chances for you to assess yourself. Each chapter will allow you to focus on one of the many aspects of the wild and wonderful world of psychic power.

Consider this book as your first step into a world of endless potential. You are at the start of an exciting journey. Let your interest in psychic matters help you envision and achieve new possibilities for yourself. We will help you discover and try out for yourself techniques such as visualization, clairvoyance, crystal ball gazing, tarot, and so on. We will give you practical and safe guidance on every aspect of psychic power and how you can experience it. You will be taken stage by stage through those hunches and vague thoughts that, when put together, make up psychic power—your silent power.

Two

Crossing a Special Line

Now it's time to start developing your psychic ability. Remember, it's not something you can do overnight—as with any skill, it takes practice. Like riding a bike, or doing algebra. Okay, maybe not like algebra. It's much cooler than that, because you're learning all about yourself.

Let's get started. In order for you to start using your psychic senses, you'll need to cross a very special line—the line between your psychic side and your nonpsychic side. Think of it like this:

The nonpsychic world	The psychic world
Your physical self— eyes, ears, nose	Your mind and spirit— your thoughts

Psychic Spotlight

Stop right now and look around. Really listen to the sounds, look at the sights, and smell the air. Life's experience is all around you and flooding in through your body's senses. Many of us take our senses for granted. But it is only when you become more aware of them that you can know when you are getting psychic information without using your physical senses.

Now, here's the trick: Crossing this line isn't as easy as walking over it. It's not something you can do with your body. You've got to do it with your mind. The funny thing is, you can't have psychic awareness without bodily awareness. The more aware you are of the physical world around you, the easier it will be for you once you step across that special line and into the world of your psychic abilities.

Psychic Spotlight

What's on the outside can also exist on the inside. Don't be afraid to look deeper.

Feeling, hearing, and seeing your thoughts is the beginning of psychic development. The idea to focus on is this: What is on the outside can also exist on the inside. That is where crossing the line begins. For example, you can imagine being in school without actually being there. Or you can think of your boyfriend or girlfriend without him or her being physically present. You can feel and see your thoughts moving in your head. They may be about what is happening in the world outside of you, but they take place inside of you.

Glimpsing the Other Side

Phew—that was tough going. Let's take a break now from all this heavy stuff and get down to some exercises involving less reading and more doing.

Psychic Exercises

The exercises in this book work well on their own, and you can do them whenever you wish, whether all together or one at a time. This isn't a textbook—you don't need to work through it, putting check marks next to things when you finish them. Remember, the exercises are not tests, and there are no right or wrong answers. Just try out the exercises and see how you feel. You may even want to go back and do them again later, once your psychic perception changes. If you think better by writing things down, take a few minutes after each exercise to jot down your perceptions, feelings, and observations. Don't worry if the exercises don't work when you first try them. Not all of the exercises are right for everyone, and you may find that some exercises suit you better than others. It may take time to catch on, so keep a positive attitude. Work with the exercises in this chapter repeatedly. Try them at different times of the day to see if you are more successful at certain times than others. Remember the first time you tried to ride a bike? You probably took a couple of spills before you got the hang of it. It's the same with psychic work—give it time and you will get there.

Wise Words

Give room to psychic thoughts and ideas— once you do, you will feel the fabric of your life change.

Psychic Cool-Down

As you know by now, you already have tons of psychic potential just waiting to be discovered. Think of the exercises in this book as psychic workouts. Just as with your regular workout, you want to do a "cool-down" once you've finished. A psychic cool-down is a simple act that brings you back to normal:

- Grabbing a snack
- Going for a walk
- Surfing the Net
- Calling a friend

Exercise: The Circle of Your Life

This exercise will help you take a look at your life and what time and space you have for psychic growth.

- Draw a circle to represent your time in a waking day.

- Now cut your day into slices that represent each area of your life—school, friends, work, homework, family, travel, time given to help others, time given to travel, and most important, time given to yourself alone. Be as honest as you can.

All finished? How'd you do? How much time do you get to yourself each day? Probably not much. Your psychic growth is about to become a section of that circle, and it's an awesome way for you to get centered and get in touch with yourself! ▲

Exercise: Thinking About Thinking
This exercise will help you organize your thoughts as you get in touch with your psychic self.

- Make a list of all of the things you think about on a daily basis—anything from love, boyfriends, and girlfriends to appearance, money, school, dreaming of the life you want—whatever crosses your mind.
- Next, draw your circle again and indicate the amount of time you spend thinking of things from your list.

Take a look at your chart. First of all, don't you do a lot of thinking? And second, you've probably noticed that most of your thoughts are traceable back to the physical world. The way you look, who likes you, who doesn't like you, how well you are doing in school, and so on. This is perfectly normal. As you advance, you'll be using your mind more and more to think thoughts that aren't so rooted in the here and now. ▲

As you work through this book you will see some really cool changes taking place. You'll begin to see that the addition of even just a few intuitive, non-sense-related thoughts, slipped in among the thousands of others, can produce the most amazing changes in your life. A large part of your absence of psychic ability till now could simply be the result of not giving mental room to psychic thoughts and ideas.

Exercise: The People in Your Life Game
This is a really cool exercise, but in order to play the People in Your Life game, you have to be in a good mood. So check the mirror and see if you look happy. No, not cheesy happy like a bad game show host, but genuinely happy—the kind of happy that comes from within. If you're having a total blah day, come back to this one later. Okay, now we're ready to play:

- First, grab a notebook and a pen.
- Write down the names of two boys and two girls that you know.
- Write down the first three songs that come into your head.
- What is your favorite animal? Describe in three words.
- What is your favorite place in the world? Describe in three words.

Okay, you've answered all of the questions. So what do they mean? Check out the key below to find out.

Key:
- The first boy/girl you thought of is likely to be the one you really like. The second boy/girl is likely to be the one who knows you best.
- The first song is what you would like your relationship with the first boy/girl you thought of to be. The second song is your state of mind at the moment. The third song is what you think of life in general.
- The qualities of your favorite animal are the qualities you look for when choosing a boyfriend/girlfriend.

- The other three words are how people would describe you.

Whatever the answers you had here, the important thing is that you think about how different people mean different things to you. ▲

Exercise: Walking Backward
Think of this as a stretching exercise for your psychic senses—the more often you do it, the more flexible and open to psychic impressions you'll become. The cool thing is, you don't have to actually walk backward—you only have to *remember* backward. This is a powerful exercise, and it's tricky at first, so don't be discouraged.

- Choose a quiet, comfortable place where you can pay attention to your thoughts and will not be interrupted.
- Take a deep breath to relax your body and prepare your mind.
- Start from this moment, and remember the events of the day backward to the moment you got up.
- If you get stuck, go back for just a chunk and then work forward to untangle yourself.

Sounds easy till you try it, huh? You probably have no problem remembering things in sequence forward from the moment you got up—but working backward is a totally different story. ▲

Psychic Spotlight
Walking backward is a very powerful way of stimulating your mind, so don't overdo it. As you think backward, don't push yourself too hard. You may only manage five- to ten-second bursts at first, but you'll soon see that a mere ten seconds every now and then is quite enough for psychic purposes.

Exercise: Tomorrow Is Another Day

This exercise will get you thinking about the future—you may even make a prediction or two! Keep a notebook nearby so you can jot down some notes when you're through.

- Choose a comfortable place where you can concentrate on your thoughts.
- Close your eyes, breathe deeply, and be sure your feet are firmly planted on the floor.
- Take a few deep breaths, then project yourself into the next day. See yourself following through on your plans for tomorrow. See, hear, feel, and taste what your day will be like. Take your time.

What did you notice? Who was with you? What were they wearing? What were they doing? If you didn't see any visual images, what did you hear? Any words? Any songs running through your head? How does your body feel? Did you smell anything?

Save your notes and read over them tomorrow night to find out if you were able to make any predictions. ▲

Exercise: Different Levels

This is a simple thinking exercise you can do anytime, anyplace.

Choose something familiar to you that you see or use every day—your coat, for example. Now you're going to think about your coat on four different levels.

Level One

First of all, think about your particular coat. What color is it? Where did you buy it? What good or bad times have you had when you wore it? In short, just think about your coat and your associations with it.

Level Two

Think of coats in general—think of all coats everywhere. Coats you have had in the past. Coats you dislike. Coats you like. How coats are made.

Level Three

Think of the purpose of coats. What do coats actually do? Why do people wear them?

Level Four

Finally, think about the quality coats have in the most abstract universal sense. For example, protection and warmth are the main features of coats. So let your thoughts focus on the image of warmth in the broadest sense. You may think of fire, or the taste of comforting warm soup. In other words, think of the idea of warmth and protection as much as you can. ▲

Exercise: Scanning

It may sound really technical, but it's not! Scanning has nothing to do with computers—it's about seeing the energy of others. It may not happen right away, but once you get the hang of it, scanning can tell you a lot about the people you meet. Here's what to do:

- When you are introduced to someone new—a classmate, a new teacher, whoever—take a moment to imagine that person as a ball of light or pure energy.
- Now scan that person from top to bottom, bottom to top, noticing any words, images, colors, thoughts, sensations in your body, anything at all, however crazy, that comes up while you are scanning.
- If you can, write these impressions down and save them. Once you have gotten to know the person better, look back at your notes. Do your first impressions fit with their lives?

We all have auras that surround us and are invisible to most people's eyes. The aura is a series of colors that reflect our mood and general energy levels. Bright colors generally show that the life force is strong and well. Dark colors show tiredness and depression. We'll check in with auras later in the book. ▲

Exercise: Places
In this exercise, you'll think about the places in your life in which you spend a lot of time—school, home, work, and so on—in order to help you observe your impressions about the world around you.

- Think about the places where you spend most of your time. Write them down.
- What places leave you with a good impression? What places leave you feeling restless or unsettled?
- Think about which places are good for you and which places aren't. You may find that certain rooms in a house or sections of a particular road are "not so good" for you. You don't need to give any reasons; don't even look for any. Simply choose a house or a school or a street in your mind and decide whether the place is good or bad.

Once you've made your observations, grab a friend and talk to them about it. You may be surprised how often other people feel the same for no reason.

Is All This Working?

Wow—you have done a lot of thinking here. The world inside your head and beyond your senses should start to become a much more real place to you.

The awareness of a world inside your head that is different from the physical world is where your psychic power will start to show itself. It's crucial that you understand at this early stage that this awareness is separate from the other thoughts and feelings that come flooding in from the outside through your senses. From now on you are going to develop a whole new way of seeing things. Your new way of seeing things isn't the world of sights and sounds and senses but a world of non-sense-related awareness or gut feeling or intuition. Gradually, a whole new world is opening for you. You can call it many things—psychic power, intuition, or sixth sense. Better yet, you could call it "me."

Three

Tuning In

What do you think so far? Have the exercises helped you open your mind? Doing these types of exercises and looking at things more spontaneously will help you gently slip across into the world of psychic possibilities, magic, and mystery.

Now that you're becoming more open to receiving psychic information, it's time to learn more about how you can receive that information. There are loads of ways to get psychic info, and each and every person has a specific way that works best for them. It's kind of like choosing a style for yourself—are you punk, alternative, or glam? Are you into designer clothes or secondhand treasures? Whatever your style, chances are you're comfortable with it—it defines you in some way. Try to think along those lines when reading the descriptions below. Just like your favorite jeans or shoes, you'll probably find that one of these methods is a perfect fit for you! It all has to do with how you process information. You can receive psychic messages through:

* Clairvoyance
* Auric sight
* Clairsentience
* Telepathy
* Hands-on healing
* Channeling
* Spirit guides

We'll explore these types of psychic awareness in a second, but before we do, try answering some of the questions below to discover the way you are most likely to receive psychic information. Don't worry if you can't say much at this stage—the aim is simply to get you thinking about how you access your psychic information.

1. When in the past have you been right about something but you had no idea why or how? It can be something important, such as a relationship not working out, or something trivial, like knowing who was calling when the phone rang. Describe that experience here:

_____

_____

_____

_____

2. Did you just get a flash of insight?
3. Did you "just know"?
4. Did you get a physical sense in your body?
5. What did your insight feel like?
6. Was your insight positive or negative?
7. Did you hear a voice in your head? If yes, what did it sound like? How was it different from your normal self-talk?
8. Did an image come to mind? If yes, what was that image? Was it real or symbolic? (For example, if the person calling was your ex-boyfriend, did you see his face or did you see a black hole?)
9. Was there a smell associated with your insight?

Understanding the way you receive psychic information is another step toward building it. No one way is better than the others, so if you "just knew" but can't describe how, don't worry. Don't feel pressured at this stage to label yourself in one category. Now that you have begun your journey of psychic exploration, who knows what psychic abilities you may discover!

Clairvoyance

Have you ever seen images in your head? Perhaps you saw yourself passing an exam before you heard that you had passed? Perhaps you saw blue flowers in your mind's eye, and when you score a date with the class

Psychic Spotlight
For some, clairvoyance is like having a movie screen inside your head.

hottie, you see at dinner that the tablecloth is decorated with little blue flowers? If you have, you might be receiving psychic impressions through *clairvoyance*. Clairvoyance comes from a French word meaning "clear seeing." It is the power to see an event or an image in the past, present, or future. But this type

of sight doesn't happen with your physical eyes—it happens with your inner eyes. A person with clairvoyant ability can receive information in the form of visual images or symbols. For some clairvoyants, it's almost like having a movie screen inside your head with images moving across it. Other clairvoyants may see symbols that they learn to interpret, or perhaps people and animals in their spirit form.

If you have strong visual skills, you may be particularly attuned to developing clairvoyance or auric sight. If you can answer yes to the questions below, you are most likely a visual person, and therefore more likely to receive psychic information through clairvoyance.

* Do you think in pictures?
* Do you most notice what things look like rather than how they sound, feel, taste, or smell?

* Do you enjoy art?
* Are you fascinated by the appearance of people, objects, or the environment?

Auric Sight

Can you easily read good and bad vibes? Do you ever associate your friends with certain colors? Do you ever see a certain color or light radiating from people around you? If so, you may have a heightened *auric sight*. Like clairvoyance, auric sight relies heavily on your visual sense.

The aura is a subtle energetic field that surrounds both living and nonliving things such as animals, plants, stones, houses, clothes . . . you get the picture. Believe it or not, even your favorite pair of shoes has its own aura!

Chances are, you've felt auras even if you couldn't see them. For example, you've probably heard people say "she's glowing" or "he gives off good vibes." These are auras in action! The information we receive from someone's aura has a profound effect on our first impression of them. Have you ever thought why some of your friends are easier to talk to than others? It's often because their aura is bright and cheerful and welcoming.

But auras aren't just about feeling— they're about seeing, too. A person with auric sight can see the positive or negative vibes from other people in the form of colors or light radiating from them.

Psychic Spotlight

All things, living and nonliving, have auras. Even your favorite pair of shoes has its own aura!

Aura Angles

If you have auric sight, you may be able to spot auras in a variety of ways:

- A subtle light appearing around a person—like a double or ghost image
- A subtle color, such as green, white, or blue
- A full range of bright, vivid colors (only if you have highly developed auric sight)

Even if you don't have auric sight right now, with practice, you can develop it. Exercises later in the book will help you on your way.

Clairaudience

Have you ever heard sounds or voices that you know are real, even though they aren't happening in the "real world"? A bell ringing, a baby crying, a song that keeps repeating itself? Have you ever been convinced that you heard someone calling you even when they weren't? Have you ever heard voices warning you not to do something or get involved with someone? Or, perhaps you've heard an insistent voice in your head telling you to do something, like approach a certain person or read a certain book and when you do a door opens for you that leads in a new and exciting direction? If you have, you may be receiving psychic impressions through *clairaudience*. Clairaudience means "clear hearing," and it is the ability to receive psychic impressions through sound.

Psychic Spotlight

When you meet someone, does a familiar song pop into your head? If so, you may be receiving a psychic message through clairaudience!

How can you tell if you process information audially? If you answer yes to any of the questions below, chances are that you have a tendency toward clairaudience.

* Are you a good listener?
* Are you good at noticing changes in tone, pitch, and frequency of noise?
* Do you describe your experiences in terms of sounds you hear or what you were listening to?
* Do you find certain sounds and noises unbearable?
* Do you have a flair for words?
* When you meet someone, does a familiar song pop into your head?

Psychic Spotlight
Do you have a "psychic ear"—an ear in which you receive your psychic impressions?

Through practice, you will be able to tell if the voices you hear are psychic information (intuition) or your own daily thoughts. A great way to figure it out is to listen carefully— your intuition speaks to you in a kind, loving, and gentle way. Self-talk tends to be a little harsher, such as "Don't forget to turn in your English term paper!" You may also find that you have a particular psychic ear—meaning that either the left or the right is the one in which you hear your psychic impressions.

Many people have some degree of clairaudience, but they don't recognize it or they take it for granted because it's always been there. You have probably always received words, thoughts, and ideas in your head without questioning their source. Lots of your good ideas may have come as a clairaudient insight. Because of what we see on TV, we often expect psychic information to arrive in a spectacular way. The truth is that we are so used to it that we don't even notice it! Open your eyes . . . open your ears . . . listen with your whole body . . . and you'll be amazed at what you'll find!

Clairsentience: Your Inner Sensing

Are you a person who trusts gut feelings? Do you sometimes know something will happen before it does? Are you an emotional person? If so, you may be receiving psychic impressions through *clairsentience*. Clairsentience is often described as clear thinking, or clear knowing. It is the most common way that people receive psychic information, especially for women, teenagers, and children, who tend to be more emotionally based than men are. As a young adult, you are quite open intuitively and emotionally. Most adults tend to shut down this aspect of their awareness.

Whether you know it or not you have probably received information in this way. For example, you meet a new classmate and feel as if you are being pulled in lots of directions. Later, when you get to know each other better, you tell her what you felt. Your new friend tells you that she is feeling run down and exhausted because her parents are divorcing and she can't decide which parent she wants to live with. Coincidence? No way!

Psychic Spotlight
Clairsentience is the most common way people receive psychic information. As a teen, it is especially common for you to have clairsentient abilities.

While it is often the stomach area where you are most aware of receiving psychic impressions, the chest, heart, and solar plexus are also very sensitive. There are lots of other types of physical knowing. For instance, mothers often experience pain or suffering with their children, husbands can experience sympathy pains for their pregnant wives, and medical psychics can also feel someone else's pain.

How can you tell if you process information emotionally? If you answer yes to any of the questions below, you probably have strong clairsentient tendencies.

* Are you empathetic and compassionate toward others?
* Are you often affected by the moods of people close to you, such as friends, parents, or brothers and sisters?
* Do you get a bad taste in your mouth when something isn't quite right?
* Do you smell things for no reason, such as roses when you are happy?

Still not sure about where you fit in? The exercise below will help you get in touch with the way you receive psychic information.

Exercise: Sunny, Happy Days
Read through the next two paragraphs. Better still, get a friend to read it to you, or record it yourself on a tape recorder and play it back.

Close your eyes and breathe deeply. Gently relax. In your mind's eye, imagine yourself on a sandy beach on a beautiful sunny day. You can smell the sea air. You hear the seagulls. A gentle breeze lifts your hair. You hear and see the waves gently lapping on the shore. You can feel the warmth of the sun on your skin. Your feet are bare and you can feel the sand between your toes. Then you bend down to touch the cool water. You hear children laughing behind you as they make sandcastles.

You walk along the beach feeling calm and relaxed and happy. You notice that you are hungry and see an ice cream stand ahead. You approach it and buy an ice-cold vanilla cone. You taste it in your mouth and feel it slide down your throat.

Now open your eyes slowly and think about what you experienced.

- Did you see the sandcastle, the ice cream stand, the sea?
- Did you use your sense of touch to feel the sand, the sea, and the vanilla ice cream?
- Could you smell the sea air?
- Could you taste your ice cream?
- Could you hear the children laughing?
- What emotions did you feel as you walked along the beach?
- Which one of your senses was easier for you to get in touch with? Which sense do you think was dominant for you?

Telepathy

Have you ever had the same thought as a friend at the same time? Have you ever sensed that your mother was mad at you before she even said a word? If so, you were experiencing *telepathy* at work.

While telepathy is a beloved sci-fi plot device in movies and on TV, the reality is very different and far more believable. In fact, we all receive psychic information in a telepathic way to some degree. We go about our lives transmitting and receiving information without being aware of it at all! Each of us is unique but the basic principle is the same: we are all like radios that can tune in to information and send out signals on certain frequencies. Some of us have a greater ability to receive; others are more able to transmit.

Your individual telepathic abilities are linked to your other psychic gifts. Use the following chart to determine how you best receive telepathic information.

Telepathic Tell-All

How are you receiving telepathic information? If you're:

- *Clairvoyant*—You'll receive telepathic information from visual images or symbols.
- *Clairaudient*—You'll receive telepathic information through thoughts or sounds.
- *Clairsentient*—You'll receive telepathic information through sensing another person's physical or emotional state.

Short-Distance Telepathy

Telepathy can operate at any distance, short or long. Without even knowing it, you have experienced short-distance telepathy with your friends and family who live nearby. Think about it. Every time you call someone you are using telepathic ability. Even though you can only hear their voice, a part of you sees their expression, tunes in to their feelings, and so on. We often pick up a range of signals that include body language, tone of voice, and expression as well as telepathic thoughts that the person transmits and we receive.

Long-Distance Telepathy

Long-distance telepathy is just as common as short-distance, though it often seems more amazing because you don't have the obvious physical signals. Perhaps you have thought about someone and a few days later you got a letter from him or her. Or maybe you thought about someone and then unexpectedly bumped into him or her.

Hands-on Healing

Do you have healing energy? Many people have the power of healing energy without even realizing they have it! Hands-on healing is a remarkable gift. It is the ability to channel a range of spiritual, magnetic, or vital energies to help others heal themselves. Often these energies are transmitted from one person to another via the hands; that's where the term "healing hands" comes from.

Psychic Spotlight
The healing energies in hands-on healing are transmitted from one person to another via your hands!

During hands-on healing, a healer may physically place his or her hands on the body of a person and allow the energy to flow through his or her hands into the area that needs to be healed.

However, physical contact isn't always necessary when using hands-on healing. Many healers work by placing their hands near the person and sending energy to where it is needed. This kind of healing is traditionally called spiritual or faith healing.

Getting Started: Hands-on Healing
So, now you know that anyone can do hands-on healing, but how? Like anything else, hands-on healing comes with practice and willingness to experiment. Think about this:

Simply thinking loving and giving and healing thoughts about someone can help that person feel more calm, peaceful, and relaxed.

Channeling

Have you ever drawn a picture, written a story, or listened to music and lost yourself to the creative muse? That's channeling. But don't be fooled—channeling is some pretty advanced stuff, and it's a skill that can only be attained once you've mastered the basics of psychic development. In the meantime, though, here are a few ways that you can channel information:

* Through mental pictures or sounds
* Through direct speech
* Through automatic writing

Your Higher Mind

We all have a higher mind or consciousness that helps to guide the course of our lives. This consciousness sees the bigger picture rather than the details we often get bogged down in. The higher mind is a part of our mind that acts as a bridge between the physical and the spiritual. Getting in touch with our higher self can help us make positive life choices and guide us in the right direction for fulfillment and happiness. The process of developing your psychic potential will automatically strengthen your connection to your higher mind. Your higher mind communicates in many ways, including sending messages to you through your psychic or intuitive senses. Good psychic work is channeled directly from your higher mind, or as we like to call it, your inner guide.

Getting in touch with your inner guide and your psychic self may seem strange and awkward at first, but the more you practice, the more you will be able to incorporate psychic abilities into your daily life. As you make contact with your inner guide, you'll be able to see some changes in yourself:

* You'll feel more calm, cool, and in control of your life.
* You'll feel more creative.

* You'll feel more productive.
* You'll feel that you can achieve even more success.

This new you won't be completely without problems. The difference is that you'll be able to handle your problems with more spunk and confidence than you ever did before.

We hope that the information in this chapter has helped you think about the different ways you may receive psychic information. Knowing which way you feel most comfortable will show you where to focus your practicing efforts. Don't get upset if it isn't immediately clear to you which method of psychic aware-ness you are drawn to. Later in the book we are going to explore things in more detail. For now just keep observing yourself and thinking about what you have read here. In time, things will start to make sense. We promise.

Psychic Spotlight

Your inner guide is the ideal you. It is your inner wisdom that guides you to be the best that you can be. It is the part of you that sees and knows all.

Four

Three Big Words:
Relaxation, Meditation,
Concentration

N ow that you're well on your way to exploring your psychic powers, it's time to take it one step further. In this chapter, you will learn to relax, concentrate, and meditate. But before you do that, you'll have to do some searching—searching for that special place in which you can do your psychic work.

Let's call this place your sacred space. Your sacred space is an actual place in the physical world that connects you to your inner spiritual world.

What Does a Sacred Space Look Like?

Sacred spaces come in all shapes and sizes. There is no "right" way to create one—just make sure you are comfortable. Check out hints for your sacred space below. Don't be afraid to use your imagination.

- Your sacred space doesn't have to be large. It can be a corner of your bedroom or your living room.
- Your sacred space can be inside or outside, depending on what is special to you.
- Your sacred space is totally portable! It could be a box with a candle and a special cloth that you carry around with you. (Hint: this comes in especially handy if you have to share your bedroom.)

Sacred spaces can be anywhere, but it is up to you to make them sacred and special. You are the one who needs to create your own bridge between worlds to create new possibilities. Creating a sacred space sets up a place to tap into your magic self.

Make Your Space

The first thing you should do once you decide upon your sacred space is to clear out the excess clutter and debris. That's right—throw away all of those old school notebooks and put your CDs back in their cases and do a bit of organizing. After all, no one wants a messy sacred space!

Once you've cleared the clutter, you can personalize your space with items that inspire you. Here are some do's and don'ts for creating your sacred space:

Do:
- Choose objects that are special to you.
- Use soft lighting or candles.
- Surround yourself with comforting sounds—a fave CD, nature sounds, or even silence.

Don't:
- Clutter your space with unnecessary objects.
- Use bright lights—they can be distracting as you try to relax.
- Bring your cell phone! Turn it off when you enter your sacred space.

In a perfect world, all of these do's and don'ts would be easy. In the real world, they're sometimes hard to accomplish. Just do the best you can—remember, these are simply guidelines; they are not essential.

Even if you can't find a quiet spot or haven, you can still practice your psychic skills anytime, anywhere.

Wherever and however you decide to work, there are two things that are important for your psychic development:

1. Relaxation 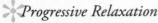 2. Grounding

Relaxation

Relaxation is important for the success of all psychic work. With so much stuff going on in your life every day—school, friends, parents, jobs—the pressure of your daily routine can keep you from understanding messages from your higher self. There are two kinds of relaxation techniques that are good for you to learn. Before you start any psychic work or exercise, you might want to begin with one of these two relaxation techniques:

1. Progressive relaxation 2. Rhythmic Breathing

Progressive Relaxation

Okay, so it may sound a little funky at first, but trust us, you'll love it! Here's how you do it:

* Make yourself comfortable, and take some slow deep breaths.
* Send warm soothing thoughts and energy to every part of your body, starting with your feet and moving up to the top of your head.
* You can do this by saying to yourself *My feet are relaxed . . . my ankles are relaxed . . . my knees are relaxed . . .* and onward to the top of your head.

This is a wonderful way to begin your psychic work, because the more relaxed you are the easier it is to get in touch with your psychic power.

Rhythmic Breathing

This is a fantastic way to relax and get in touch with yourself. It's all about counting to five. Give this a try:

* Begin slow rhythmic breathing from your stomach, breathing naturally but slowly.
* Inhale through your nostrils for a count of five.
* Hold for a count of five and then exhale slowly for a count of five.
* Imagine and feel warm energy flowing through your body. Feel the pause of peacefulness in between each breath.

You can use these methods to relax anytime—before a big test, after a long day, or even if you can't get to sleep at night.

Grounding

When you finish your psychic exercises, you need to "ground" yourself—return to your daily life and reconnect with the physical world. Grounding can be different for everyone, so here are some examples of how you might ground yourself:

* Try some stretches to reinvigorate yourself.
* Make a cup of tea.
* Eat a snack.
* Call a friend.
* Write down your magical experiences in your journal.

Psychic Spotlight

Keeping a journal is a great grounding exercise. Besides helping you keep in touch with yourself, it's a great way to track your psychic progression. The more you learn, the more you'll have to write about!

Sounds like a lot to remember, doesn't it? Don't freak—the list below will help you review the steps you'll need for every psychic exercise.

Psychic Popup

Here's a quick list to help you remember what to do before, during, and after your psychic exercises.

- Perfect Prep: Setting the Mood
    - Find a time to yourself—no cell phones, no interruptions.
    - Set the tone any way you like—play soft music or light candles.

- Real Relaxation
    - Relaxing is important—don't forget to do either *progressive relaxation* or *rhythmic breathing* exercises.

- Other-Worldly Workout
    - Do your psychic exercise.

- Reconnection and Reflection
    - Always end with a grounding ritual—write in your journal, talk with a friend—whatever you need to do to reconnect with the physical world.

Concentration

Another vital ingredient for success in your psychic work is concentration. Without the ability to concentrate in your psychic work, you won't make much progress.

What Is Concentration?

Concentration is the ability to focus on a chosen project and ignore what is irrelevant.

There are some key words in that definition. Concentration requires you to choose a project from the many others requiring your attention. Then you must have the discipline to ignore all else. In other words, if you are doing a psychic exercise recommended in this book and thinking about the hottie in math class, or your term paper, you're definitely not concentrating!

Psychic Spotlight

Chris Evert Lloyd, the famous tennis player, taught herself how to concentrate. When she was practicing under the hot Florida sun she would force herself to stay on the court hitting balls even when she was tired or the sun got in her eyes. It paid off for her time after time. After winning a major championship a reporter asked her if the noisy planes flying overhead had bothered her. She looked back at him and replied, "What planes?" She had so totally focused her mind on the game that she had become oblivious to the outside world!

Think of a time when you were so focused on what you were doing that you were able to block out distractions. Write about it in your journal, if you like. Try to think of how you felt at that time. How can you re-create that when you are doing your psychic exercises?

Don't think you can? Think again! This exercise will help you improve your concentration and get into even better psychic shape.

Get Ready!

Before you begin any psychic exercise, make sure that you aren't tired or hungry. Then remove as many distractions as you can. Wait until you have done your schoolwork or called your friends for the evening. Find a quiet spot if you can. Okay—now you're ready!

Exercise: Concentration Creation

This is such a powerful exercise for your psychic development that you might want to practice it every day.

1. Sit in a relaxed and upright position in a chair that is comfortable, but not *too* comfortable.

2. Mentally prepare yourself for your psychic work. Tell yourself that you are "goooood" at concentrating. By repeating "I'm gooooood at concentrating," you are already learning how to concentrate and are developing the belief that you have this skill.

You can repeat these words in whatever way suits you best. If you love to read, write the words down and read them over and over again. If you enjoy talking, say them over and over again. If you enjoy writing, write them over and over again.

3. Now, give your mind a two-minute assignment. Tell it that you are going to read, write, or say "I'm goooood at concentration" for about five minutes. Tell it that you'll think about nothing else but those words. Don't try to concentrate—just do your assignment. Be careful that you're not scrunching up your face or hunching your shoulders like you do when you take a test. Just set your alarm for two minutes,

then start the exercise with all of your attention. Before long, you will be concentrating!

4. The first few times you try it, you might start thinking of other things—like what you're going to wear to school tomorrow, or whether you'll get a good grade on that paper you turned in today. It's okay—concentration, like anything else, takes practice. Just remember that you are the one who controls what goes on in your mind. You have the power to control what you think about. As soon as you become aware that you are thinking about something else, simply stop, say "no," and return to your assignment with greater intensity.

5. When you are able to concentrate for two whole minutes without being distracted, try increasing to three, four, and then five minutes. Then introduce distractions. Turn on the radio, keep your eyes open, sit in a room with your family. Repeat the exercise with distractions until you are able to concentrate for five minutes without having things compete for your attention.

This exercise takes most people three or four weeks to master, so don't worry if you don't get the hang of it right away. Once you are ready to concentrate your mind, you are ready to transfer these skills to psychic development. ▲

Psychic Tips

Here are some tips to get you back on track if you're having trouble concentrating:

- Read the thought you wrote down with exaggerated head movements.
- Speak louder so your mind is fully occupied and less likely to wander.
- Don't get upset or impatient with yourself—just be patient and persist!

Psychic Spotlight

Your mind will always have a tendency to wander. Don't give up! Try not to force things or feel tense. If you start to feel tense, take a break. You can always come back to these exercises later.

Learning to Meditate

Okay, so now you've learned why concentration is important to psychic development. And the ultimate form of concentration is *meditation*.

Many people talk about how great meditation is, but if you haven't tried it you may ask, "What's the big deal?" In fact, with your life being so busy, taking time to meditate seems odd. But when you take time to meditate you really aren't doing "nothing." Meditation can recharge you, reduce stress and anxiety so you gain a calmer and more peaceful approach to life, help you tap into your psychic power, and assist you in finding a source of creative ideas. If you still feel weird about the term *meditation*, try thinking of this as a time for stillness, quiet, or even prayer. It really doesn't matter what you call it—just give it a try. Many people find it easiest to meditate before they begin their day. Others like to practice at the end of the day. Try different times to see what works best for you. Just be sure to choose a time when you are least likely to be disturbed.

Psychic Spotlight

Meditation helps you receive intuitive guidance because it puts you in a state of mind in which you are relaxed and less likely to be distracted. Over time a daily meditation of ten to fifteen minutes will work wonders for your psychic development.

There are many different ways to meditate. So what is the right way? Keep your cool! It isn't always those who try the hardest who get the best results. Sometimes those who do not try too hard to get it right end up doing the best. Just start your concentration exercises in a positive frame of mind and then trust yourself to do the best that you can. Don't force things.

At its simplest meditation can be divided into two forms.

1. Stillness
2. Thoughts and images

Stillness

By concentrating on stillness and giving your mind something to think about, you distract it from the thoughts and confusions of daily life. For example, to still your busy mind, try focusing on the movement of your breath, in and out, counting each exhalation.

Thoughts and Images

The second kind of meditation is more specific. It offers particular thoughts and images, as you did in the concentration exercise earlier in this chapter, to stimulate your mind as well as relax it. Both kinds of meditation are useful for developing your psychic potential, and both are helped by deep breathing. Breathe from your stomach, not your chest, and slow down both your inhalation and your exhalation.

Most of the exercises that follow in this book are written to guide you through a set of ideas and to stimulate your psychic senses. It would be really helpful if before each exercise you did a couple of minutes of gentle breathing, and made a conscious decision to relax and settle your mind.

Psychic Spotlight

Why not imagine that each thought that enters your mind turns into a beautiful bird or butterfly before flying away, leaving you calm, clear, and still?

Exercise: Your First Meditation

And now first let us prepare the ground for the exercises to come with this simple meditation.

- Sit or lie down in your sacred space. Most people prefer to sit upright, but if you prefer lying down that is fine—as long as you are not the kind of person who is likely to fall asleep whenever you lie down!
- Make sure that your back is supported or straight and that your body is open—that means don't cross your arms and legs. If you are physically open, you are more likely to be emotionally open, too.
- Once you feel comfortable, allow your eyes to close. Breathe deeply in long, slow breaths, filling your lungs completely, gently holding the breath for a moment, then releasing the air.
- As you breathe, silently tell yourself that you are willing to develop your psychic potential. Allow your fears, doubts, and negative thoughts to dissolve into a haze of golden light.
- Now picture yourself standing in a doorway that glows with golden light. Imagine that you are surrounded by light energy. Tell yourself that you are safe. Tell yourself that you will listen to your intuition and act with love and compassion.
- Imagine that you can smell flowers and hear the sounds of beautiful music. The feeling of this place on the other side of

the door is bright and inviting; you know that you are standing on the threshold of your unique psychic potential.

- When you feel ready, see yourself stepping through this doorway and finding yourself on the other side, bathed in even brighter golden light and feeling warm and comfortable. The sounds and smells are even sweeter. The ground beneath your feet is soft but firm. You feel secure and stable. Stay here for a while, enjoying the feeling of this place. If you get any particular ideas or thoughts, take note of what they are but don't dwell on them.
- When you are ready, gently stretch your body and open your eyes, sitting quietly for a few moments before getting back to daily life. ▲

Congratulations! You've just completed your first meditation. The more you meditate, the more naturally it will come to you.

Exercise: Psychic Senses Meditation
Here's a meditation that can really help you connect with your psychic senses.

- Sit on a chair with your back straight and shoulders relaxed. Fold your arms on your lap and close your eyes. Take three slow breaths. Inhale and exhale deeply.
- Imagine that your whole body is filled with light. Picture every cell being bathed in white light that fills you with peace. This light holds all the wisdom and love from the universe. See the light completely filling you and surrounding you.
- For five to ten minutes, pay attention to your breathing. Watch it in your mind's eye going in and out of your body. If your

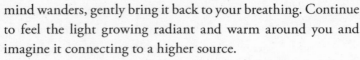

mind wanders, gently bring it back to your breathing. Continue to feel the light growing radiant and warm around you and imagine it connecting to a higher source.

- Ask your intuition if there is a message for you, and listen for an answer. You may also ask for guidance on an issue about which you need insight, or say a prayer for a person or a situation.

- End your meditation by visualizing the light being sent to a person or situation that needs help. Some people like to say "thank you" at the end, or "amen." ▲

Many people find that they can't easily focus when they try to meditate. If you're having a hard time concentrating, try one of these techniques. However you choose to meditate, don't worry—there is no right or wrong way. It's a very personal thing to do, and whatever works for you is best.

Mandalas

Mandalas are a beautiful way to help you meditate. These beautiful, usually circular designs draw your eye to their center, which helps your mind focus. When creating a mandala, the artist tries to coordinate his or her life circle with the universal circle, reflecting how each life fits into the larger whole and how our inner and outer selves can unite.

Psychic Spotlight

Mandala is Sanskrit for "circle." It refers not to the shape of the circle itself, but to the circle of life.

Mantras

If the visual doesn't do it for you, try the sound-oriented approach—use a mantra during meditation. A mantra is a sound, word, or phrase that you repeat to keep your mind focused. The sound is intended to resonate in the body and evoke certain energies during meditation. The Hebrew word *shalom* (peace) is commonly used as a mantra. Other frequently used words are "om," "love," "beauty," "peace," and "God." Any word that is sacred to you or evokes a special feeling or a quality you seek to develop is a good one to try out.

Still Can't Concentrate?

By now you know that concentration is crucial for your psychic development. But what if you find it virtually impossible to concentrate or relax? Don't worry—you aren't alone! Here are some comments from other teens who are having trouble concentrating.

> "I really want to develop my psychic gifts, and I've tried many times to sit and meditate and focus my energy, but I find it really hard to stop thinking about what has gone on in the day. I can't stop the chatter inside my head. Either that or I get so relaxed I fall asleep. I just don't seem to be able to concentrate." —Tina, 15

> "I think I could be good at this psychic stuff, as I'm really interested in it, but I always have so much to do and think about—homework, chores, friends, basketball, my girlfriend— that I can't clear a space in my head." —Clay, 17

Let's face it. Life can be so full of pressures—pressures from family, friends, and school—it's no wonder it's tough to concentrate. That's why the next chapter is all about finding ways to help you get the focus that is crucial for success, not just in psychic development but in the rest of life, too.

Five

The Power of Imagination

By now, you know that in order to strengthen your psychic ability, you have to trust your imagination.

Imagination is the foundation for psychic development. It is your imagination that will take you on your first psychic adventure. Most of us neglect our imagination, but imagination is the key to everything you do. It's a natural human sense and it needs training.

To develop psychically you need to allow yourself to dream, fantasize, and play. The trick here is getting there before your rational mind can sort, assess, and figure out what to do.

Of course, being rational is important, but when you're doing your psychic work, it's all about your imagination. This chapter will help you develop creative ways to use your imagination and strengthen your psychic powers.

Picture This

Here's a great example of how imagination can influence your psychic ability.

Psychic Spotlight

Imagination is the ability to picture things that are not visible around you. It is the ability to mentally see an image of whatever you want rather than what is imposed by the outside world.

After a hard day delivering lunch and dinner orders, a pizza-shop employee drives past an abandoned shop. In a flash he sees it as it could be—a cool restaurant. As he peers through the dirty glass windows he can see diners talking, laughing, and eating. Several months later he asks his bank to loan him the money, and the project is under way—all because of a flash of imagination!

Psychic Spotlight

Your imagination has its own language—pictures and images. The next time you get a flash or idea in your mind, pay attention! It could be your psychic powers trying to tell you something.

Can you think of a time when a flash of imagination inspired you to try something new? Perhaps you looked at your bedroom and in a flash saw it in a different way. With permission from your parents and a bit of paint, you had a whole new room.

Strengthening your imagination is the way toward psychic insight. To understand your imagination, you need to think in pictures and images. Words are not the language of your imagination. So how can you strengthen your imagination? This chapter will give you lots of ways to help you strengthen your imagination muscles.

Trust Your Imagination

To give yourself permission to use your imagination, here are some daily *affirmations* you might want to use.

Psychic Spotlight

Affirmations are simple, powerful statements that gently help you alter beliefs, habits, and expectations that are helpful in developing your intuition. The development of your intuition will always help you with your psychic development.

The more you use affirmations, the more effective they will be in helping you develop your psychic power. You can use your affirmations anytime, anywhere—from first thing in the morning to last thing at night.

Imagination Affirmation

I trust the power of my imagination.

It is safe for me to develop my intuition.

I am a creative, imaginative, and intuitive person.

I trust my gut feelings and reactions.

I can use my psychic gifts with ease.

Psychic Insight

At this stage we are going to steer clear of psychic work that involves predicting the future. It's the area of psychic ability that gets the most press, but it's also the area that requires the most careful handling and experience to practice. As you know by now, being psychic does not mean having the answers to other people's problems. Knowing about other people and their affairs is one tiny aspect of being psychic—and there's a lot of responsibility involved. Are you ready to:

* Be a counselor to others?
* Be questioned constantly by friends and acquaintances about their futures?

Chances are, you're probably not. Before you start predicting the future for others, there's a much more common and easy ability to develop—using psychic power to learn about yourself.

If you've been doing the exercises in this book, you probably have lots of ideas about what you'd like to do with your new abilities. So let's experiment with some real psychic techniques.

How do you gain psychic insight? There are two simple steps:

1. Abandon words and ideas as your main way of thinking.
2. Call upon the powers of your imagination and your intuition.

Getting Your Imagination Going

There is no better tool to get your psychic awareness ready to roll than the Tarot deck. Whether you're familiar with the Tarot or not, this section will help you to understand it better and teach you to use it. If you don't have one already, you might want to pick up a deck before you continue.

Tarot cards are the forerunners of modern playing cards. The deck consists of seventy-eight cards divided into two groups: the Minor Arcana (fifty-six cards) and the Major Arcana (twenty-two cards). There are four suits in each deck:

1. Pentacles
2. Swords
3. Cups
4. Wands

Psychic Spotlight

Think of Tarot cards as picture books for adults. The Tarot card experience is completely visual—it will help to inspire feelings.

Tarot cards are a lot like picture books. Think back to when you were a kid and your mom or dad read you stories. While you remember hearing their voices telling the stories, what you probably remember most is the pictures—the details of the story and the feelings they bring up. Whether it was the setting sun or the princess's hair or toy trains, the picture was real to you. You were absorbed by it. For a few moments you were swept away by the story, living in your imagination.

Tarot cards work the same way. By looking at them for a few moments you begin to notice feelings inside yourself that feel both familiar and new at the same time. This is a sign that you are making contact with psychic ability.

If you want to find out more about the Tarot cards as tools for self-development and psychic growth, check out another one of our books, *Teen Tarot*, also published by Adams Media. Tarot decks are widely available at bookstores. If you're looking for a deck, try the Rider Waite deck. It's a good deck to get started with. For now, just take a look at the cards from your Tarot deck. Fan it out in front of you.

Psychic Spotlight

Working with the images of the Tarot can be a start on the road to psychic insight. Browse through in your own way, whenever you can, and you will start to see results.

You will see before you a blaze of shapes, images, signs, symbols, flowers, weapons, animals, monsters, angels, and planets. Pay attention to the way the cards make you feel. Look at the pictures in a quiet and reflective manner. Hold on to these feelings for a few moments. Can you tell the difference between Tarot-inspired feelings and the feelings of your daily life? Emotional reactions to the illustrations are a sign that the cards are working their magic—they are getting through to your psychic center via your imagination.

Psychic Question

"Is reading Tarot cards dangerous?" —Josh, 14

Psychic ability is natural to us all, and the Tarot is simply one of many tools to help you tap into this natural ability and bring it out. People only fear the cards because the pictures of some decks look strange and mysterious. Don't worry—the cards are completely safe. If you stick with the traditional Rider Waite pack or a pack with the theme of angels, fairies, animals, and other familiar images, you won't feel uncomfortable.

Exercise: From A to B

While other exercises helped to stimulate your imagination from the outside, this exercise helps you take the step toward imagination.

- Look at these two shapes above. Cover up shape B and look at shape A.
- In your mind's eye, let shape A transform itself into shape B. See the line dividing and turning outwards.
- Try it again, only this time see one arm growing faster than the other. Do it again and see one arm waiting for the other to complete before it moves. See in your mind's eye one of the arms moving and when it stops, see the other moving.

Creative Visualization

When you imagine or visualize something, you see mental images or pictures, and those images have meanings. Visualization is important because psychic messages often come to us in pictures. Your job is to find out what the pictures are trying to tell you. Sometimes it can be difficult to understand the pictures you get.

Picture Perfect

The pictures you get can have very different meanings. Sometimes it pays to look closely—but beware of looking *too* closely!

Example: You see an image of yourself tottering down the road in extremely high (extremely fashionable) heels. You're trying desperately to keep your balance, but you end up falling down.

Meaning #1: You are about to have difficulties in an area of your life.

Meaning #2: Your heels are too high!

The more you work with your psychic power, the easier it will be for you to understand the images that come to you. This will keep you from confusing the trivial with the profound.

At the back of this book there is a list of some of the most common images and symbols that you might experience. That will help get you thinking along the right lines.

You are about to enter a new dimension of your psychic journey—visualizing images in your own head. Only you can see the images you create, and what you create in your mind can be anything you want it to be. A tree in your head could start as a tree and end up as something completely different.

The best way to work on visualization skills is to practice. Here are some exercises to help you do that. Be sure to go to your sacred space when you do your exercises so you won't be disturbed. At first you might think that you can't see anything. Just keep trying, and you will succeed. Anyone can visualize with a bit of patience.

Psychic Spotlight
The process of deliberately trying to see things in your mind's eye is called *visualization*.

Exercise: The Cross

- Close your eyes and imagine a cross—any kind of cross that you like.
- Hold this image in your mind and slowly rotate it until it is upside down.
- Continue to rotate it until it has gone round a full 360 degrees and is upright again. ▲

When you have finished, leave your cross upright. You should always leave your visualization as you find it; if you don't, you might feel a little bit uneven yourself.

Exercise: Wobbly Star

- Close your eyes and think of a five-pointed star.
- Holding this image in your mind, drape it with flowers and gently wobble it from side to side.
- Now return it to its upright position and let the flowers dissolve. Don't forget to tidy up and leave things as you found them. ▲

Live Your Dreams

As you work more and more with visualization, you will be able to visualize your future. You will be able to keep your mind on what you want to such a degree that you will actually see the future happening here and now.

Let's give it a try. Think about an event coming up that's important to you. Maybe you have an exam next week, and your goal is to do your best on it. Just follow these steps.

Get Comfy

Get comfortable and make sure you are somewhere quiet. Sit or lie down, but don't get so comfortable that you fall asleep. It might help to listen to some quiet, relaxing music through headphones to cut down on outside noise.

Psychic Spotlight

Music is helpful to relaxation, but it is not essential!

Slow It Down

Slow down your breathing and take deeper breaths. Empty your lungs by breathing out, and at the same time press gently on your diaphragm (just below your chest and above your abdomen). Now inhale slowly and deeply through your nose. You should feel this area rising and then sinking again as you breathe out through your mouth. Do this a few times until you are satisfied that your breathing is slower, deeper, and more rhythmic than usual.

Psychic Spotlight

Remember—breathe in through your nose . . . and out through your mouth. Pay attention to the rhythm and slow down your breathing.

Relax

Now tell yourself to relax the main parts of your body. For example, say to yourself, "My feet are relaxed." Pause, then say "My legs are relaxed," and so on. Relax your lower back, your shoulders, your legs, your elbows, your wrists . . . you get the picture. Relax all the way to the very top of your head!

Let Yourself Wander

Take a deep breath, and as you slowly pull it in, feel a tingling sensation run all the way down your body from the top of your head to the tips of your toes. Now spend a few moments just listening to the silent air around you, and let your imagination go where it will. You are now in a state of mental and physical relaxation, and you can start visualizing your goal. See and hear future things as if they are happening now—as if you have already achieved your goal. See yourself working hard to prepare for the exam, doing well in the exam, knowing the answers, getting great results. Try to intensify your vision and bring the whole range of senses into your imagination.

Now tap in to your psychic power. Give your plans over to the higher, positive power you believe in.

Psychic Spotlight

The positive images you created during visualization will remain with you for as long as you need them to.

Cool-Down

You are now ready to bring yourself back to normal wakeful state. It is a good idea to count slowly to ten as you do this.

Time Travel

You can use these relaxation techniques for looking back as well as forward. Suppose, for example, you really want to try out for the school play. Problem is, you have terrible stage fright because you totally choked during the school play back in the second grade and your classmates teased you unmercifully.

By using visualization, you can travel back in time and address your leftover hurts and fears so they don't bug you anymore.

As you start to visualize, tell yourself that if at any time you feel too distressed, you can come out of your sequence instantly. This is like a panic button: if it's there you feel reassured and will probably never have to use it. Now try these time travel steps.

Put on Your Traveling Shoes

Try to create an image of yourself actually traveling, perhaps in a time machine or along a beam of light.

Be Nice!

As you travel back in time, be sure to greet the person who hurt you in a friendly manner. Now explain that his or her actions during your childhood were very hurtful and damaging to your development. Did the person know this, or was he or she just being tactless or insensitive? Go into specific details of your experience here. If at any time you feel intimidated, just push your panic button.

Forgive and Forget

If it becomes obvious in your visualization that the person never intended to hurt you and never even realized that damage was done, explain that the situation did cause you unhappiness. In the end, make sure you forgive him or her. Make a promise to yourself that you are no longer going to allow the damage or hurt to continue. If the person did want to hurt you, just tell yourself that the past is done and you are in control of yourself. If you want to try out for the school play, no one can stop you but you!

Psychic Spotlight

Still afraid? If your panic button is out of order, try imagining the person as a cartoon character.

Leave It All Behind

You are now leaving all your feelings of hurt, anger, and resentment in the past, where they will drift away in the mists of time. When you return from your imaginary journey you will not only have cast off the pain of the past; you actually will have turned it to your advantage, and you will be a more understanding and sensitive person.

Exercise: The Think-About Game

Okay, now it's time for a fun exercise. All you have to do is grab your journal or a piece of paper.

Part One

Write down the first three words that come to mind for each of the images below. The first three words are usually the best—don't think about it too hard!

• Waterfall

• White (the color)

Part Two

Which one of these shapes do you like the best?

circle   cross

spiral   triangle   square

Answers:

- Your feelings about the waterfall may reflect your attitude toward the opposite sex.
  - Do you have a crush on someone?
  - Are you just getting over a breakup?

If your answers made you laugh, why not have some fun and ask your friends this question too. You don't have to tell them why you are asking the question.

- The color white represents eternity.
  - If your feelings toward the color white are negative, then the future is something that you feel apprehensive about.
  - If your feelings are positive, then you are looking forward to it and not daunted by what might be in store for you.

- The shape you chose tells you a bit about your personality.
  - If you chose a circle, you are very independent.
  - If you chose a cross, relationships are essential to your happiness.
  - If you chose a spiral, growth and change are important at the moment.
  - If you chose a triangle, you are practical and precise.
  - If you chose a square, you value stability, or need it in your life. ▲

These exercises all tell you something about yourself. Don't get upset if you didn't like your answers. Life is about constant change. There is an old saying that tells us you can never step in the same river twice. The reason that's true is because a river is always changing, and the water is always flowing. Try to think of your life in this way. Who you are now may be nothing like who you are in five years. For example, if you are shy about asking someone out, in a few years' time you may have more dates than you know what to do with.

You Again

Okay, let's tune in to your imagination once again and unlock some more of your secrets. Be sure to use the A to Z guide at the back of the book if you need help interpreting images. Remember: don't think about your answers too much—just feel! This section will help you discover important things about yourself and the way you see the world.

The Path Game

Picture yourself going down a path. It can be any type of path you like—a path in the woods, a path in your town, even a familiar street. Imagine the path and hold that image in your mind.

You come across something in your path that keeps you from continuing. What is it? What lies ahead of it? What do these answers say about you?

Your Path/Your Life

The path you imagined is how you see life. Each person will imagine his or her path as something different. Here are some path possibilities.

Bumpy

If you see a bumpy path, then you see life as a bit of a bumpy ride. Perhaps you've had a rough time at school or at home? Don't worry—life is full of the good and the bad, and things can always get better.

Straight

If you see a smooth, straight path, then your life has been very smooth up until now. You feel happy, centered, and you've got it together.

Winding

If you see a winding path, then you may be a very secretive person. You tend to keep to yourself, and you are careful about who you trust.

Into the Distance

If your path stretches far out into the distance, you are probably a very direct person. You're always honest. You speak your mind, and you have very little to hide.

Know Your Obstacles

Okay, now that you know a bit more about what your path says about you, let's take a look at obstacles along your path. Once you identify your obstacles, you can overcome them. Did any of these images pop up in your path? Here's what they could mean:

* A wall suggests that you tend to keep your feelings to yourself.
* A small mound means that you can cope with whatever is thrown at you.
* A large rock is a big issue that you have to face and conquer.
* A wild animal means that something is scaring you from moving on with your life.
* A fallen tree could be an emotional problem.

See the World Around You

What did the scenery around the path look like? Here are some explanations of what it could mean:

* If the scenery was lush and gorgeous, then life is yours for the taking!
* If the scenery was desolate and gray, you may be scared of what the future has in store for you.
* If the scenery was foggy or unclear, then you may not know what to expect from life yet. No worries, though. You've got plenty of time to figure it out!

One Girl's Reaction

Jade, age 15, felt a little sad when she completed the Path Game. Here's what she told us: "I see a dusty road going downhill in a gentle slope. I want to be an actress. I know what I want to do but the dust means my dream may be unrealistic. I get depressed at times, so I think that going downhill means going nowhere. The obstacle in my path is a big bear. She looks just like my mother. My mother is sick all the time and I am always looking after her."

Picture Perfect

This is really fun to do. Check it out and see what you think!

Pretty As a Picture

First, you have to choose a picture you like. It can be a photo or a painting or a drawing. Try to pick something calm or uplifting rather than something scary. Also, make sure your picture isn't crowded with too many things. After all, you want to relax and chill out!

Psychic Spotlight

Remember—think carefully about what you want and set your goals to get there. Life is yours for the taking!

Find a Space

Find a place (preferably your sacred space) where no one else is around and you are not going to be disturbed—where you can go to relax. Take the picture with you.

Get Comfy

Now it's time to get comfy. Here's how:

* Wear your favorite comfy clothes, like your softest pajama pants or jeans.
* Sit in your favorite comfy position a few feet away from the picture.
* Take several deep breaths to relax.

Take a Good Look

Tune out everything else that's on your mind and look at your picture for a few minutes. Try to memorize every detail in the picture. Here are some things to look for:

* Where is everything placed in the picture?
* What colors are there in the picture?
* What image from the picture jumps out at you the most?

Close Your Eyes

When you're ready, close your eyes and try to remember everything in the picture. Here's how:

* Describe the picture to yourself. Mention every detail, however small.
* Try to see the picture in both words and images.

✳ See the picture in all its glorious detail. Perhaps the picture is even better in your head than in real life!

Look Again

Now open your eyes and take a second look at the picture. Look at everything in great detail.

✳ What did you remember?

✳ What did you forget?

✳ How many different colors were there? You will be surprised at how quickly you forget things.

If you've forgotten a ton of stuff, try going back to the first step and doing it again.

Go for It!

Now that you've had a good look, it's time to really have some fun.

Psychic Spotlight

Don't be afraid to use your imagination during the Picture Perfect exercise! Your imagination is what makes your experience so special.

✳ Close your eyes and imagine that you are slowly melting into the picture.

✳ Stand in your imagined picture, look at everything, and see it all in your head.

✳ Take a walk in your picture. Enjoy it.

Be Open

Don't be embarrassed or afraid to interact with your picture. No one is watching but you, so be as open as you can! As you walk around in your picture, try doing these things:

* If there are people in your picture, start a conversation with them.
* Enjoy the mood of the picture—feel it in every part of your body.
* When you feel ready, slowly walk out of the picture and come back to reality.

Ground Yourself

Take your time coming back to reality. Once you've returned, take a few moments to ground yourself with some of the tips you read earlier. These earthbound activities after an exercise are as important as the exercise itself.

Two More to Try

The final exercises in this chapter should only be repeated one or two times. We don't really want you to think much about them; just observe. Both are designed to help develop your imagination and the feeling you have for your inner world. So simply watch for the pleasantly unexpected in these exercises, and then get on with your life. All the benefits will follow without your even knowing it.

Exercise: Candle Meditation

This is a simple, relaxing meditation. Remember—sit back and enjoy, but don't think about it too much. Here's what to do:

* Go to your sacred space or a quiet room and turn the lights off.
* Take a white candle and put it in a holder. When you feel calm, light the candle.

- Now watch the flame of the candle carefully for about a minute. Blow out the candle and make sure it is completely out.
- Close your eyes and look at the image on your retina. Focus on it and eliminate any other thoughts. Let your attention rest there for as long as there is anything left to look at.
- After five minutes or so, open your eyes, relight the candle, and prepare to re-enter the normal world. Turn on the lights. If you can, let your candle burn for a while before you blow it out again.

Exercise: Color Visions

Here's another great meditation. Remember—these are all about impressions, so try not to think too much! Here's what you do:

- Cut out a five-inch square piece of white paper.
- Using a felt-tip pen, draw a circle and color it blue. Now color around that circle in orange.
- Look at this card for about two minutes. Don't force yourself— just keep your eyes focused on the card for as long as you can.
- Now close your eyes. You will see a faint likeness of it in your inner vision, although the colors might change. Watch this inner image until it fades. Make no attempt to change it.
- Try to do this every day for five days. After a while you should find that you can see the card clearly in your mind whenever you want. All you'll have to do is close your eyes and wait!
- Keep doing this for another week or so. Then one day, when you see the card with your eyes closed, simply open your eyes. The image may not disappear, but will be hanging there suspended in space—a vision.

Six

Clairsentience: Pushing the Boundaries

As you've already learned, psychic power is really a natural extension of an ability we all have—intuition. Your intuition tells you to call your best friend, and when you do, you find out she's just been dumped. Or you think of an old friend for no reason at all, and he or she suddenly comes back into your life. When we talk about intuition, instinct, gut feelings, hunches, and so on, we are referring to one distinct area of psychic awareness, the skill of *clairsentience*.

Clairsentience is the ability to get intuitive insight and information through your sense of touch or feeling what is around you. It is also the best place to start when you embark upon your psychic adventure. If you sharpen your ability to notice and respond to your gut feelings and instincts, you create a firm foundation for the development of other psychic skills.

Psychic Spotlight

Clairsentience is possibly the most common of all psychic abilities, yet it is the least recognized and acknowledged.

This chapter contains some ideas, exercises, and practical techniques that can enhance clairsentient awareness. You may well find that what you learn here will enhance your other psychic gifts, such as clairvoyance and auric sight, which we will discuss later.

Gut Feelings

The term *gut feeling* isn't accidental. The area of the body between the heart and groin, which consists of the stomach and solar plexus, is particularly sensitive and said to have its own intelligence—hence, gut feelings!

Psychic Spotlight

Our gut is where we often experience a feeling for the environment we are in. Think about it. If you walk into a place with an unhappy vibe, you'll probably leave feeling uneasy. But if you spend time with someone who is genuinely kind, it leaves you with a warm glow.

Exercise: Gut Meditation

Okay, time to do another meditation. This one will help you learn more about your gut instincts.

- Find a quiet place and get relaxed. Breathe deeply, allowing each breath to fill your lungs completely without straining. Exhale slowly.
- Imagine that the area just below the center of your rib cage has a mind in it that steadily vibrates. Imagine that every feeling you have exists because of this mind.
- Now think about what your emotions are telling you. Are you calm, excited, sad, turbulent, joyful? Do your best to notice all that you are feeling, and let your feelings ebb and flow at their own pace.
- Now imagine your solar plexus and stomach filling with colored light that looks like bright sunshine filled with softness and warmth, making you feel at ease within your body.

- Relax your stomach muscles and let that feeling of energy spread to every part of your body. Sense the energy of this light touching you deeply to awaken your intuition.
- Now your gut awareness is stimulated to receive information. You are strengthening your innate clairsentience.

Psychic Touch

Did you know that your skin is your largest sensory organ? And the energy surrounding your skin is your aura, which is the mostly invisible blend of energy around every living thing. Your skin and your aura work together to register everything you come into contact with, no matter how subtle. While most of what your skin and your aura pick up gets easily lost, you can easily learn to pay attention to what you feel around you.

Psychic Spotlight

An aura is an energy field that surrounds the human body. Auras can be many different colors, and vary from person to person.

About Auras

It may sound crazy, but your body gives off light, sound, electricity, and even magnetic frequencies. All of these intense energies form the human aura. The qualities of this energy field are largely responsible for clairsentience.

Aura Exchanges

Energy exchange through the aura doesn't just occur between people. Here are some other auras you may come into contact with:

- Plants
- Animals
- Objects
- Places

You exchange energy with the people you meet every single day. Think about it: If you've been around a lot of people you will have exchanged a lot of energy and will feel quite tired. You may even have a few strange thoughts running about in your head. This is totally normal. Picking up and giving off energy is called *imprinting*. Developing your clairsentient ability will help you learn to read these imprints.

If you've ever moved to a new town or changed schools, you know that it takes a while for a new place to feel like home. This is because it takes time for you to imprint your energy on it. The longer and more direct your contact with something, the greater the imprint you will leave. A good psychic will be able to pick up on that. For example, can't you tell when your kid sister or a friend has been messing with your stuff?

Psychic Spotlight

Did you know that the aura is predominantly electromagnetic? We are constantly giving off energy and absorbing it through our auras.

Tune In to Touch

Your aura is your own personal energy imprint. No two auras are ever alike because each one of us is unique. In the following section and exercise you will learn to read imprints by focusing on holding an object that belongs to someone. This is a psychic technique known as *psychometry*, and it can be used to help you learn more about a person.

When you tune in to an object or a place, you're asking your inner guide to pass information on to you. One way it does this is to stimulate physical sensations. It may also stir up emotions within you or create images in your mind relating to the imprints on the object.

Here are some ways your inner guide may help you receive imprints.

times, and as you do, pay attention to what you feel or sense. You may feel pressure building between your hands. You may feel a tickling sensation or sense a warming up or cooling down between your hands. ▲

After learning to energize your hands and stimulate their sensitivity, you can take things one step further.

✳ Energize your hands and then hold one of your hands over the forearm of the other and move it back and forth without touching.

✳ Do you sense any energy surrounding your forearm? Try other parts of your body, and if a partner is willing to work with you, try doing the same with them.

✳ This is just to get you used to sensing your energy field and, if you work with someone else, their energy field.

Exercise: Psychometry Sensations
Now that you've tried some other exercises, let's try psychometry—reading energy imprints from objects.

• Ask some of your friends to bring small objects, and then place them in envelopes so you have no idea what belongs to whom.

• First, energize your hands. Then choose an envelope and take the object out.

• Close your eyes and relax. Try to attune yourself to the object in your hands by paying attention to the physical, emotional, and visual sensations that come to you.

• Start with the physical sensations. Do you feel hot, cold, or itchy? Does a part of your body tingle or come to mind?

- Next, concentrate on your emotions.
- Finally, concentrate on whatever images come to mind.

When you have finished sensing everything, you can write down all your impressions on the envelope. Share your experience with the owner of the object. Get as much detail and feedback as you can. Don't worry if you didn't get anything right. This isn't a contest. The goal is to practice and have fun! ▲

The best way to develop psychic ability is to practice, but there is no reason why you can't have fun doing it. Here are some games you might like to play alone or with others.

Exercise: Sensing the Color of a Card

This is a simple game for you to play. All you need is a deck of ordinary playing cards, and you're good to go! You're going to try to sense the colors of the suit without looking at the card. Each color has its own energy or feel.

- Energize your hands. Then take one black card and turn it face up. Place your hands over it, close your eyes, and pay attention to what you feel.
- Repeat with a red card.
- Now choose one card and keep it face down. Try to feel if the card is red or black.
- Turn the card over and see if you were correct. Repeat with another card. You'll be surprised at how quickly you improve!

Sensing Atmospheres

Everything that happens within an environment affects the way that it feels, and can be registered by those with clairsentient ability. You may like or dislike how a room looks or smells, but part of you is also picking up how it feels. For example, a room that is loved or cared for will feel quite different from a room that is neglected.

There is also a difference between a room that is used by people who relate to each other well and a room where there is bitterness.

Psychic Spotlight

With feng shui, the placing of certain objects such as mirrors, lights, and so on can all help regulate negative energy.

Practitioners of the art of feng shui know a lot about the need to balance energies in an environment. A balanced environment becomes a healthier and more harmonious place for people to live and work in. Feng shui is the ancient Chinese art of tuning in to the seasonal changes and vibrations of nature to bring you health and happiness.

Clairsentients work in a similar way, but rather than follow a particular system, such as feng shui, they instinctively know how to bring harmony to their surroundings. They may suggest colors, shapes, or objects that can transform the feeling of an environment. Good clairsentient awareness of environments also can help to keep us safe. If we walk into a building and receive a gut feeling that something isn't right, we can make good choices about our well-being—where we live, where we work, and so on.

Exercise: A Drop in the Ocean

This exercise is a fantasy meditation that is designed to stimulate your environmental awareness.

- Sit or lie down comfortably, either in your sacred space or another quiet atmosphere.

- Breathe deeply and imagine yourself to be a beautiful fish in an ocean. Enjoy the feeling of freedom as you glide through the water.
- Now imagine yourself to be one fish among a school of many brightly colored fish. You swim in rhythm with your group. You sense their mood and shift your direction in perfect time and rhythm with the others.
- Now take this one step further and imagine yourself to be able to feel the mood of the entire oceanic world. You automatically sense and locate where to feed, play, and swim, and where you'll be safe. You are in total harmony and fully attuned to your ocean world. ▲

Wouldn't it be amazing if you could sense, read, and respond to the environments you live and work in? Think about the difference an awakened clairvoyant sense is going to make to your life!

Exercise: Getting to Know a Room

This next game is designed to help you detect feelings and atmospheres surrounding you.

- Walk around a room in your house (not your bedroom) and notice everything about it.
  - How light or dark is it?
  - What colors are in it?
  - What shapes?
  - How warm or cold is it?
  - What sounds can you hear?
  - What does it smell like?

- Next put your hand on your stomach and notice how you feel. How do you feel about this room? Give yourself plenty of time to think about it.
  - Is this area relaxed or tense?
  - Does the room have a personality?
  - Is there a happy atmosphere?
  - Are the people who use this room happy, or is there stress?
  - Has anything happened in the past in this room that is still influencing the present?
  - Trust your gut instinct to give you answers. If the room does not feel balanced, ask yourself what needs to change to improve the atmosphere. You may want to take notes of your impressions and compare them with those you may have in the same location at another time. As we keep saying, the best results come with practice.

In Tune with Your Room

If you spend a lot of time in a place or room but don't feel comfortable with it, there are many things you can try to change the feeling. Be inventive and use sensual images that are appropriate for you. Visualize positive people and experiences coming into your room. Here are some quick redecorating tips:

- Rearrange your furniture.
- Hang pictures on the walls.
- Imagine a force field of your favorite sounds, feelings, and smells surrounding your room.

Gut Instincts About People

Of course, your gut instincts can tell you a lot about a person, but there's a fine line between clairsentient ability and prejudice, so you must be careful! With regular practice and a willingness to have an open mind, we can all learn to have a more accurate first impression of other people.

It is generally healthier to take a positive view of other people when you first meet them because you are more likely to find positive qualities in other people if you look for them rather than anticipating the worst. However, sometimes you just get a sense that it is safe to get close to someone, and sometimes you get nagging feelings of doubt. Always listen to your gut instincts.

Trust Your Gut!

Here is sixteen-year-old Jenny's experience with another girl:

> From the first moment that I met her I just got this sense that I couldn't trust her. But she was really pretty and everyone else seemed to get along with her so we used to hang out together in the mall at weekends. She always seemed to be more interested in our friendship than I was and I was flattered. Six months later I found out that she was making out with my boyfriend. When I confronted her she told me that she only hung out with me so that she could see what the competition was like. It made me feel sick. My gut instincts were right.

Receiving clairsentient information about someone isn't all black and white—it's more than just a positive or a negative reaction. Clairsentient information can take the form of landscapes, colors, textures, feelings, and sensations. Here are some examples of the forms clairsentient information may take:

* You sense the mood of your best friend before she gets to school.
* You experience a fluttering in your stomach at the exact moment your friend breaks her arm.
* You may find that you sense the feelings of joy, sadness, excitement, and loss before the person who is experiencing them tells you about them.

We all radiate a vast amount of information about ourselves and the experiences that have left an impression on us. We all have a level of clairsentient ability that helps to keep us safe and helps us relate better with those around us. Psychics simply use this clairsentient information to help them guide and support others to make the most of their talents and abilities.

Empathy

Psychic Spotlight

Empathy is feeling what someone else feels, or seeing things from their point of view.

Have you ever imagined what it would be like to be someone else? Have you ever taken on the attitudes and behaviors of someone else—maybe a best friend or someone you looked up to?

You can develop empathy so strongly that just by touching someone you can feel and experience what they do. Be careful, though. Some people are more naturally empathetic than others, so you do need to be careful about becoming too sensitive. We'll explore this more later in the book.

A Psychic Look at Our Bodies

Don't worry . . . this isn't anything like biology class! While we often look at the body as a complex medical system, we'll take a different approach here. Let's try looking at the body in separate sections. By taking a psychic view of the body, you will learn to read and understand people better.

The Head

Have you ever watched someone nodding off to sleep in a car or train? The head drops . . . then they wake . . . and the head comes up again. It's a battle for the head to stay on top. The head likes to think of itself as the king of the castle, and in many ways it is.

Psychic Spotlight

Heads together! The next time you are with a group of people, just be aware of their heads. Watch how the heads move. If you copy the way someone else's head moves, you may be able to generate inside you a tiny feeling of the emotions that person may be feeling.

Arms, Hands, and Voice

Your arms, hands, and voice all perform an extremely complex dance of gestures and sounds. The next time you speak with a stranger, try to concentrate on his or her movements and voice. Can you detect patterns and harmonies? Can you tell what kind of mood the person is in?

Many psychics need nothing more than a voice in order to gain impressions. Pay attention to those around you. Can you tell how they are feeling? Here's a list of feelings you might be able to sense just from watching and listening:

* Happy
* Sad
* Genuine
* Nervous
* Aggressive
* Soft

The whole character of a person is in the sounds that they utter—it doesn't matter what they say. So tune up your inner sensitivity to the max and really listen. What emotions are floating around in the voice? Think of words like these to describe the feeling behind the voice:

* Warm
* Anxious
* Proud
* Impatient
* Doubtful

People's normal everyday voices, even when they are saying "pass the sugar please," are full of such emotions. If you are a visual kind of person, you may even want to close your eyes and listen intently to "see" how that voice appears in your mind's eye. What shapes can you see? What colors can you see? What images?

The Trunk

Now it's time to think about the trunk—the heart, lungs, spine, and intestines. Your spine strives to hold everything together. It plays a great part in the struggle upward.

What kind of messages come from the trunk region? Check out the following game to find out.

Five Steps Forward, Five Steps Back

This game is to help you get in touch with your trunk and learn what it might be trying to tell you.

- Stand with your back against a wall.
- Take five steps forward.
- Take five steps backward, paying close attention to the feelings in your middle and your back.
- At step four, you may become aware of a distinctly different impulse building within your middle and your back.

Psychic Spotlight

To become aware of your heart-lung rhythm, simply feel your pulse beat. This feeling of the lifeblood coursing through you with every breath is a link with the great mystery of existence.

Diaphragm

Your body has what is called a *passage time.* That's the time it takes for liquid to pass through your digestive system and out. Most of us put things in at one end and make little connection between that and what comes out of the other. So drink some cranberry juice and note the time when your urine takes on a pinkish hue. This will give you some insight into the timing of one of the basic rhythms of your body. Believe us, there are psychic lessons and feelings to be experienced from bodily sensations!

Psychic Spotlight

Being psychic is not just an experience for your head—it's an experience for your whole body!

Hips and Pelvis

The area of your hips and pelvis has an energy all its own. It deals in part with reproduction and the whole cycle of bringing new life into the world. It is a subtle and powerful energy, and you can feel it by simply giving your hips a wiggle.

Stomach

Your stomach is an extremely vital psychic center. Later on, when you use your power to sense other people, you will become aware of this very sensitive area.

Legs

Think about how you walk. Watch what other people do with their legs. Keep watching, and you'll find that leg movements can speak volumes about a person. Try to copy the way someone else walks, or step in time with her or him. This can bring on powerful feelings of being tuned in with the person.

Feet

Ever hear the phrase, "Put yourself in my shoes"? Your foot is your connection to the earth, and your body's energies flow through and from the ground beneath you. It's amazing how putting on a new pair of shoes or the shoes of someone you know can give you a different feel.

If you want to understand someone better, imagine their shoes in front of you and step into them.

We hope that this section has helped you think of the human body in a psychic way. There is a whole world of meaning in the human body that can touch and inspire your growing psychic perceptions of yourself and other people.

Now it's time for some games to help you understand the movements and feelings of the human body.

Exercise: People-Watching

Do you remember what empathy is? Empathy is feeling what someone else feels, or seeing things from their point of view. Developing your empathetic feelings can help you enhance your psychic ability. You can work at developing these feelings anywhere, anytime.

- Go to a public spot, and look for a person you can observe without being noticed.
- Now imagine that you are that person. What would it be like?
- How is he or she feeling? What would it be like to be that person?

In time you will find it easy to read people more accurately. You will be able to see past the masks people wear.

Exercise: Exploring Someone

It's best to do this exercise first with a person you know well, but when you are comfortable with the technique you can use it for new people.

- Ask someone you know well to sit opposite you. Hold the person's hands and close your eyes. Pay attention to your heart and stomach, and notice the sensations you experience.
- Breathe deeply and begin to sense information about that other person for about ten minutes or so. Take this opportunity to explore any other feelings that are there.
- Take your time—it takes a while for the information to filter through.

- When you feel ready, open your eyes and share the information you received. Deliver the information as positively as you can.
- If you have tapped into an area that the person doesn't feel comfortable discussing, don't go there. Instead, shift to other impressions that you had.
- To complete the exercise, move away from the other person and imagine yourself harmlessly breathing out all the feelings that are not yours and do not belong to you.

You may be surprised by how much you learn from this exercise. Chances are, you received far more information about the other person than you realized.

Psychic Spotlight

Don't forget to ground yourself at the end of all of your exercises! Do something usual and earthy to ground you, such as moving a chair to its original place or gently rearranging the lighting.

Seven

Awaken to an Inner World

unches are the building blocks of your psychic development, and just like things in the physical world, they follow certain patterns. Just as the food you eat nourishes your body, your feelings are food for your inner world, and some foods are better for you than others. A diet of self-interest, competitiveness, frustration, and boredom will not produce a strong psychic sense.

There is one special "feeling food" that you'll need more than anything else, both in life and in developing your psychic senses. What is it? Respect. Believe it or not, respect for life, nature, and the amazing world we live in—combined with wonder and awe—is the richest food to stimulate your psychic growth.

Psychic Spotlight

What is respect? It is your willingness to express your appreciation; it is holding others in high regard, no matter what.

Psychic Change of Gear

Why are we talking about respect now, and why is this important? Cast your mind back to our earlier discussion about how simple mental challenges can be triggers to psychic growth. This is what we are trying to do again here.

By holding the idea of respect in your head now and again as you work, you will give yourself a psychic change of gear. Your understanding will step up enormously. If you're having trouble grasping this, think back to when you were a child. Was there someone who inspired awe in you? If that doesn't help, think of spectacular things in the natural world—a waterfall, a rainbow, a sunset—that inspire awe. By tapping into your feelings of awe, wonder, and respect, you will step up a gear psychically.

Honesty Is Always the Best Policy

What goes hand-in-hand with respect? You've got it—honesty. As your psychic abilities grow stronger, it's soooo important for you to be open and honest. Always do your best! As you read this book, you are awakening to an amazing inner world. But for you to have happiness and success in both your inner and outer worlds, your motives have to be pure. Some sayings are worth repeating . . . and honesty is definitely the best policy.

Try to work through the rest of this book with these ideas of respect and pure intention at the back of your mind. You'll soon find that feelings of awe and respect come naturally, and along with them comes a desire to do the right thing.

The information in this chapter will encourage you to see the messages within the natural that can arouse your psychic senses. It will also prep you for the more advanced work in future chapters—clairvoyance and clairaudience.

Growing and Declining

You can learn a lot about the world around you by paying attention to things in nature that are in the process of growing, beginning, or

flourishing. Pay equal attention to natural things that are decaying and withering away. For example, you could focus on these things:

* Flowers growing in a box.
* A playful kitten or puppy.
* Leaves falling from the trees. In this case, the pattern is one of growing and fading . . . living and dying. It's the universal life cycle.

Psychic Glimmers

Ready to give your growing psychic powers a try? Let's do it!

- Imagine that you are walking to school or a friend's house, and you notice a blossoming bough on a tree.
- Tune in to the life cycle and think of growing and fading.
- After a day of doing this you will start to notice specific feelings within yourself. You may notice that you get the same feeling from the growing things you see. Chances are, you get the same feeling from the fading things you see, too.

By concentrating on growing, a feeling a bit like the sun rising happens. By concentrating on fading, a feeling of the sun setting might occur. Now hold on to these feelings and really feel them. They are real glimmerings of psychic awareness. They may be dim and distant right now, but in time they will grow stronger.

If you pay very close attention to the feelings of growing and fading, something incredible will happen. You will suddenly feel as if you are part of an energy force that passes through and around you. You may not be able to see it, but you know that it is there. The energy you are feeling is as real as anything in the material world. You are simply tuning in to something that is nonphysical. And the more we work together as you read through this book, the more you will get to know these forces.

Psychic Visions

Now things are starting to get exciting! Now that you can feel these growing and fading energy forces, it's time to get to know them and see them in a psychic way. Take a deep breath. You are now ready to experience the beginning of psychic vision.

This is a completely new way of looking, so give yourself time to get into it.

By now, you have found out that growth and decay had certain feelings, images, lines, and shapes associated with them. Start to look for very specific images, lines, shapes, forms, or patterns that surround these two forces. Tune in to the feelings of each energy force and start to imagine growth-type shapes and decay-type shapes. What you are trying to do is connect the feelings of the forces you have been thinking about with the shapes that surround them. We are not going to tell you what shapes or lines to look for—you need to see them psychically yourself, and come to your own conclusions.

It might be hard at first, but keep trying. Soon you will get what we mean. It's almost as if you have to ignore the thing you are looking at until you get the feeling of growth or decay associated with it. Then you can really start to concentrate on it and see what lines, patterns, and shapes come to mind. It sounds much more complicated than it is—honest.

Psychic Spotlight

As you develop your psychic visions, you will begin to feel a new way of seeing things rather than just letting your eyes rest on them. You will start to see the essence of things.

Once you have gotten used to the feelings and shapes of growth and decay, try to tune in to one of them even when you don't have an object in front of you to inspire the feeling. Keeping your eyes open, try to visualize the kind of form this feeling would take if you could see it in the physical world. From now on, growth and decay won't be just words to you; they will be living forces or entities that evoke images in your mind. Congratulations! This is the start of psychic vision.

Wow! We've been doing some pretty heavy stuff in this chapter. Let's pause for a bit. Before going on to psychic hearing, you may want to rest for a day or so to keep from tiring out!

Psychic Hearing

You may not realize it, but your ears can convey feelings to you as well. Think about your favorite song. Doesn't it always make you feel a certain way?

Let's apply that to the sounds of the world around you. Listen to the sounds all around you right now.

Distinguish between sounds that are produced by lifeless things, like a bell ringing or a door slamming, and sounds that come from living things, such as animal or human sound. (Hint: We mean natural human sounds here—not the TV, your cell phone, or the radio!)

* What feeling does a lifeless sound, like a ringing phone, inspire in you?
* What feeling does a sound from a living thing inspire in you?

Unlocking Insight

The sound from living things is the key to psychic insight. Here's how you do it:

- Notice what the sound tells you, and try to bridge the gap and unite yourself with that feeling.
- It doesn't matter whether you like or dislike the sound—just try to connect with it. Fill yourself inwardly with the feeling being experienced by the living thing that made that noise.

By doing this, a new kind of hearing begins to grow within you. You develop the ability to merge with another being, and great insight can come from doing this.

This new ability to be sensitive to sound can spread throughout your whole life. You are starting to hear directly with your emotions and your thoughts rather than your ears. Natural sounds can affect you deeply, and all sound can become a source of considerable information about the feelings and motivations of whatever made it. Things begin to speak to you not through words, but through noise and sound.

Exercise: Seeing Red

After all this abstract stuff you need something simple and down to earth. Gather up some colored cards or colored paper, making sure you have red, blue, green, yellow, and any other color you like. Now hold the card of your choice up to your face in good light so you see nothing but the color on the card. Concentrate. What feelings does the color inspire in you? What feelings fit the color? Do this for each card, and then ask yourself these questions:

- Can you feel the color red in any part of your body?
- What feeling is connected with the color green?
- What feeling did you like the most from the colors you looked at?

Get to know the feelings within you that the colors inspire. If you can't concentrate, try this:

- Look at the card in front of you, and then close your eyes to explore the feelings it inspires.
- Hold the color in your mind. Repeat.

If you feel silly staring at a piece of colored card, remind yourself that learning about the feelings you get from colors will come in very handy later when we start to develop your ability to see auras and psychic colors.

Exercise: Animal and Mineral

This exercise will help you become more aware of psychic insights stirring within you. Try not to get impatient if you don't feel you are getting anywhere! Great understanding and awareness won't appear overnight. It is gained gradually, and it will stay with you forever.

For this exercise we'd like you to focus on two things in nature: an animal and a crystal.

- Find a crystal, perhaps on a ring or necklace. If you don't have a crystal, your birthstone will do. If you don't have that, try getting a lump of mineral matter such as mud.
- Now try to observe an animal—anything at all. It could be a bird or a cat.
- Compare the mineral with the animal.

What you'll notice:

- Each has its own form.

- Notice that two distinct sensations occur in you as a result of looking at the crystal and the animal.

At first you will only get a glimmer of these impressions, but in time they will grow into a feeling that stays with you and you can summon at will. It is from these impressions that you start to build your psychic sight. You might like to connect colors to the animal or crystal. What colors do they make you think of? Did the animal make you feel the color red, the stone the color blue?

You will get results from this exercise if you persist, so don't give up after the second attempt!

Exercise: Staring at a Plant

For this exercise, again designed to awaken your psychic vision, we would like you to stare at a plant. No, this isn't as silly as it seems. This exercise may in fact be the hardest one in the book so far, so don't get discouraged if you don't get immediate results.

- Observe the plant closely. Notice the color, shape, and texture. Let this thought fill your mind: "From this plant a bigger plant will grow."
- Picture in your mind a bigger plant that will grow from this plant—see what it will someday become. In other words . . . try to see the plant's future!

This exercise isn't easy, but it's really important. In time you may start to see what looks like a lilac film or cloud surrounding the plant. It isn't the staring that produces this effect; it is your understanding that every living thing is surrounded by energy. If you really can't see anything yet, don't worry. Just thinking about this idea will help enormously with your psychic development.

Sleep

Every time you snuggle up in bed and drift off to sleep you are in fact crossing over a mysterious threshold. Many of us have heard of dramatic-sounding psychic terms such as *trance mediumship, out of body,* and so on. Sure, these things may sound a little weird, but did you know that you already experience these states every night?

Psychic Spotlight

Sleep is probably something you take for granted—something that you have to do. But it's also an important part of your psychic development. Get ready to turn your brain around and look at sleep in a new light!

The hours that we spend sleeping make up a part of our lives that is totally mysterious to us. In fact, most of us blank it out or don't count it as part of our consciousness. The result is that we perceive only part of what is happening to us, or part of our awareness. To develop your psychic awareness further you will need to become fully aware of all your existence—including the time you spend sleeping.

The Power of the Moon

The moon is the ruler of the kingdom of night. For most of us the moon is just this thing up in the sky that we see from time to time. In truth, the moon has a profound and rhythmic movement, and we would like you to turn your attention to that. The more you start to notice all the details of the moon and stars, the more a force from within you will rise to the surface as psychic insight.

Dreaming

Your dream life can be more dramatic and interesting than your waking life. You get to do incredible things: fly, travel to exotic lands, meet new people, appear onstage, even walk down a street naked. Dreams are a rich source of experience, and even when they are at their most ridiculous, they are real enough to think about.

Scientists tell us that dreaming is essential to our health and well-being because our dreams act as safety valves, releasing frustration, anxieties, and feelings. But dreams can also do much more. They can:

* Organize and make sense of what happened in the day, helping us realize what's bothering us.
* Help us solve problems and overcome obstacles.
* Show us things we might otherwise have missed.
* Help us make sense of the past, restore physical and mental balance, and allow us to have fun playing out fantasies and desires.

The amazing thing is that all this goes on whether we are conscious of it or not. When you become more aware of your dreams, you can begin to see the benefits more clearly and can even teach yourself to make your dreams work for you.

Psychic Spotlight

You are the dreamer and the dream all rolled up into one incredible human being.

But what do our dreams mean? When we interpret our dreams it's like cracking a code, because the information presented in them is made up of images and symbols. The images are personal to you. They are your own thoughts, ideas, or feelings turned into a series of pictures that make sense to you. For example, if you feel confused, you could have a dream about being lost in a dark wood.

✳ *Dream Messages*

Dreaming is an exciting experience, and you can bring something from it into your waking life—an understanding, an insight, or even a tiny thought. You never know what messages are trying to come through in your dreams . . . until you start to pay attention to them.

Lisa's Dream

Lisa was going through a difficult time. Her parents had been arguing for years and finally were getting divorced. Glad that the shouting and bad feelings were going to stop, she was nevertheless upset about the breakup of the family and the changes that lay ahead. The night her mother told her the news about the divorce, Lisa dreamed she was walking down a rocky path with nettles stinging her legs. She was sad and tearful. When she had dried her tears she looked up and saw a beautiful garden filled with lovely flowers. Suddenly she felt happier than she had for months, and woke up feeling calm and peaceful.

Our dreams are often messages showing us what is in store. In Lisa's dream the life she currently has is like the rocky path—difficult and full of pain. But the dream goes on to show that despite her current sadness, the divorce will work out for the best and there will be happier times ahead.

Psychic Spotlight

An old tradition says that by day you hurl questions at the sun, and by night the moon answers. So if you want to get something out of your dream life, you must first put something in. Try asking a question of your dreams at night before you fall asleep, and believe that your dreams will supply you with an answer.

As you wander around in dreamland, the things you see are the images you are creating. Your dream is created by your own awareness. The tricky part is that things in dreams can be the reverse of what they are in real life. Here are a few things for you to think about:

* In dreams, things start at the end and work backward toward the beginning.
* Also, the things that you say in dreams are really things that you ought to hear from someone in your waking life. The things that you hear someone else saying in a dream actually are thoughts coming from you.

Confused? Don't worry! Dreams are a minefield for interpretation. Don't take to heart the well-meant interpretations from other people. The only person who can ever make sense of a dream is you. It is the inside knowledge hidden deep within you that you have to bring to your dream interpretation.

Psychic Spotlight

The best technique for understanding dreams is to request a dream in response to a wish. When your dream comes in this way you will naturally understand it. Remember—your dream is your creation, and looks to you as its creator.

What Your Dreams Are Telling You

The process of understanding involves asking yourself questions and listening to the answers that come. Relate to the dream as if it were a person whom you suddenly found in your house. You must find out what it wants. Most dreams have something to say to you—that is their purpose. Ask it questions like those that follow. Read through these and see if any of them relate to your dream in some way.

* What are you telling me about school?
* What are you telling me about my boyfriend or girlfriend?
* What are you saying about my attitude toward my parents?
* What possibilities about my future are you pointing to?
* Are you telling me about my personality?
* What are you telling me about my past?
* Are you showing me a mistake I made?
* Are you showing me my fears?
* Are you telling me to make a change?
* Are you talking to me about my friends?

Don't forget, though, that in the backward world of dreams the answer may arrive even before the question is asked, so what happens in your dream before your question may help you learn what the dream is about.

What Does It Mean?

Check out this dream example so you can learn to request and interpret your dreams:

You request a dream to tell if you can trust your boyfriend. You dream that you fall off a cliff, and then you see your boyfriend running away. Clearly this is a sign that a part of you feels that your boyfriend isn't someone that you can turn to for support in a crisis.

Your Dream Diary

What if you don't remember your dreams? Most of us forget our dreams every night. Don't just trust your memory and hope for the best; keep a dream diary. If you keep up with your diary, you'll be amazed at how your dream recall will gradually improve and develop.

Keeping a Dream Diary

Here are some hints to get you started on your dream diary:

- Keep a pen and paper or your psychic journal beside your bed, and record any dreams as soon as you wake up.
- Try to put your dream pieces together as if they were a puzzle.
- Try to remember your dream backward, from the moment the dream ended to the moment it began.
- Don't just keep a record for a few nights; make it a regular thing. Sometimes you may dream about events days, months, or years before they happen!
- Remember—when working with dreams, don't forget to ground yourself and return to your waking world.

If you get stuck with interpretation, the A to Z glossary of images and symbols at the back of this book might prompt your memory or trigger a line of thought.

Dream Incubation

You can turn your dreams into creative and helpful experiences. This process is called *dream incubation*. Dream incubation means that you get your waking mind to work with your sleeping mind. It takes time to perfect, but once you get the hang of it you'll find the whole experience mind-blowing. Here are some tips to get started:

* Decide what question you want to ask your dream. Keep things simple at first, like where to find something you have lost or how to solve a particular problem.

* Write down the question as if you were talking to your best friend—because that is just what you are doing. You are communicating with a higher part of yourself.

* Read this question over and over again and keep it in your mind during the day and again as you get ready for bed. (Don't do this exercise after watching a late-night movie!)

* Once in bed, read over your question again and ask your dream self to bring you the answer during your sleep. Then just relax, with your pen and notebook or your psychic journal ready by your bed. What you are doing here is giving your dream a task.

Technicolor Dreams

Dreaming with the influence of color can bring you many benefits. You can request certain colors in your dreams by thinking of them before you go to sleep. Different colors can bring you different things. Check out this list to learn more.

* **Green:** Nature's color for soothing and healing. If you aren't feeling well, think and breathe green to get your body's natural healing process started.

* **Violet:** Helps you to relax. If you're feeling stressed, imagine yourself surrounded with this color, and you will feel harmony.

* **Rainbow:** Happiness and good fortune. Imagine you are standing at the edge of a rainbow and let the colors shimmer around you. You might even imagine a pot of gold!

Clairvoyance and Auric Sight

eople often call someone who gives psychic readings a "clairvoyant." But there really are many different types of clairvoyance. In this chapter you'll learn simple ways to awaken your own clairvoyant vision. Even if you are not naturally visual in your psychic ability, the exercises in this chapter still will be useful.

As you learned earlier, when we first start to develop our psychic powers, we experience events through whichever of our five senses is the strongest. All of our senses work together, and it is best to start with the sense that is the strongest for you. After that, the other psychic senses will catch up.

Psychic Spotlight

Though "clairvoyant" literally means "clear seeing," it has become a catchall for various types of psychic phenomenon.

Clairvoyance means psychic ability that is based upon seeing. A true clairvoyant will receive psychic messages or information through a heightened visual awareness. They may also have other psychic abilities, such as clairsentience, but their chief source of information tends to be visual. Most teens demonstrate clairvoyant ability without even knowing it. Do any of these sound familiar?

＊ Everything went blank, and then I got all these images.
＊ I saw colors around her.

* I dreamed about this.
* I knew that she wasn't telling the truth.
* I know about this, but I have no idea why or how.

No matter what age you are, it can be hard to trust your psychic intuition. It can be quite scary. But psychic intuition teaches us that the world is not only black and white. Suddenly we see things beside, behind, in front, and all around us. Psychic vision challenges our secure boundaries and prompts us to question things.

There are two forms of psychic vision. Neither is better than the other. They are just different. They are:

1. Internal vision
2. External vision

Your Mind's Eye

Many clairvoyants get their insight internally—through their mind's eye. They may see images, symbols, and impressions that they then interpret. Seeing with your mind's eye is also called *subjective clairvoyance*.

Psychic Spotlight

Receiving impressions through clairvoyance is like watching a movie in your head. Sometimes just a thought passes through or nudges you. Dreams are also a part of this internal vision.

Subjective clairvoyance can come in several forms:

* Lights
* Images
* Symbols

However, some clairvoyants describe the images as being projected forward from their "third eye," as if there were a television or movie screen a few inches in front of their forehead. The third eye, or inner eye, gives the ability to see or sense something without using physical eyesight.

We all have the ability to develop subjective clairvoyance, although some of us may have greater natural abilities that relate to other psychic senses. No matter what your abilities are, you can learn and grow from exercising your inner eye and awakening your higher vision.

Exercise: Opening Your Inner Eye

Try this exercise as often as you can, spending time in a relaxed but receptive state so that any visual information transmitted to you from your higher mind can come through. It is a great exercise to do last thing at night before you go to sleep.

- Find somewhere comfortable to work. Breathe deeply and focus on the middle of your forehead. Imagine it as a closed eye.
- When you are ready, imagine the gentle golden light of psychic awareness awakening your third eye like sunshine opening a flower. Take a good look at your third eye.
- What color is it? Let your vision become clearer. Do you see anything? Don't worry if you don't. Just be aware of any thoughts, feelings, and sensations as you do this.
- To complete this exercise, bathe your third eye with blue light to protect it, heal it, and keep it healthy and safe, and then imagine the eyelid slowly closing. It's just as important to close your psychic power as it is to open it!

Visualization—Practice Makes Perfect

You've already begun improving your visualization skills. Now it's time to take it one step further. Here are some fast, fun ways to improve your visualization skills.

Visualize Objects

Practice closing your eyes and visualizing objects around you in as much detail as possible. This lays a foundation for psychic vision.

A Different Look at Your Bedroom

Close your eyes and make a mental list of everything in your bedroom, and see in your mind's eye where these things are. Then create a picture of your room in your head.

A Different Look at You!

Visualize the inside of yourself. Create an inner smile. Visualize each of your organs as happy and joyous.

People Peeping

Practice people-watching. What can you see inside the other person? Pay attention to everything that you feel and everything you imagine. Remember that imagination is a way of seeing.

Ring-a-Ling

The next time the phone rings, close your eyes and try to visualize who is calling before you answer. What first pops into your mind? If nothing comes to mind, ask yourself questions: Male? Female? Relative? Friend? Partial answers do count. If you thought it was your mom calling but it was your aunt, you still knew it was a female, and that's a great start.

☀ *So Many Ways to Visualize*

Aside from those we've mentioned, there are endless ways to visualize! Here are some other quickies you can try anytime, anywhere:

* When you get a present or package, try to imagine what is inside.
* When someone comes to the door, try to visualize who it is before answering.
* In the morning before heading out to school, try to picture what your favorite teacher will be wearing.

Exercise: Be a Problem-Solver

If you're having a problem, this exercise may help you.

* Close your eyes and think of your problem.
* Visualize a doorway in front of you, and then see yourself stepping through that doorway.
* You are standing in a great library. Around you from floor to ceiling are bookshelves filled with rows and rows of volumes. Here is all the knowledge of the world. There is a soft noise behind you, and you turn.
* There stands your librarian, who smiles and asks, "'May I help you find something?" You tell the librarian what your problem is. She nods and smiles knowingly and tells you that by asking your question you are beginning to find your answer already.
* She then says, "'Follow me. I think I know what you want." You wander through the maze of books until the librarian stops, reaches for a book, and hands it to you saying, "I think this has the answer that you seek." You look at the book and see that it applies to your problem.

- You thank the librarian and follow her back to the doorway. You step back into your room, bringing the answers with you. You are filled with confidence that you will know the answers soon.

Watch what happens in the next day or two. Your answer will come to you. It may come as an insight or as advice from a friend or even in the form of a dream, but it will come. You will see and know what to do.

What Do You Want?

Taking five or ten minutes at roughly the same time each day to be alone and to relax may support your psychic growth.

Psychic Spotlight

The more you can practice your inner vision, the clearer that vision will be for receiving clairvoyant information. It is also useful to send a clear message of intent to your higher mind.

However you decide to work, it is useful to begin with some daily declarations and a guided meditation with a strong visual element. As with all things in life, you are more likely to get what you want if you ask for it.

As you work you may want to ask something like:

* What do I most need to learn about myself right now?
* I would like some guidance to improve my relationship with _____ or the situation involving _____.
* I now wish to receive guidance from my higher awareness.

Exercise: Meditation to Visualize Your Clairvoyance

One way to strengthen and accelerate your development is to imagine that you are fully competent, confident, and skilled already. This is useful in mastering any new skill, such as learning to paint, draw, or ride a bike. Psychic ability is no different. The meditation that follows allows you to visualize yourself as a fully developed clairvoyant.

- Find somewhere quiet, and get comfortable.
- Imagine a future time when you are a fully developed clairvoyant. Your ability to see clearly and interpret what you see with wisdom, humor, and compassion is inspirational to everyone around you. Your abilities have brought you joy and peace of mind.
- In your mind's eye imagine what you would look like. Would you dress differently? Would you act differently? Paint a mental picture of your future self.
- Now try asking your future self for messages of support or guidance. Take note of any visual thoughts, images, and impressions that may come to you. Whether or not anything comes to you, thank your future self.
- Finally, imagine a beam of light being sent from your future self penetrating your third eye to stimulate your clairvoyant vision, and imagine yourself growing in psychic awareness.
- Imagine that you have the ability to receive detailed clairvoyant images and that your vision has a positive influence on you and the world around you. Know that you already embody the qualities and gifts of the future.
- Open your third eye even wider to give an overview of your life, your purpose, and your goals. Be aware of any inspirational images you receive. When you are ready, close your inner eye and return to normal. ▲

Objective Clairvoyance

Have you ever caught a glimpse of something out of the corner of your eye, only to discover it isn't there? Have you ever seen someone who has died or who is somewhere else?

If you have, you might be an objective clairvoyant.

Psychic Spotlight

An *objective clairvoyant* will see people, animals, and objects in spirit form as if they were physically present. *Subjective clairvoyants* see things internally, but objective clairvoyants see them in the environment around them.

Don't be alarmed if you haven't experienced this—objective clairvoyance is rare. Visions of this nature are linked to messages of wisdom or encouragement, and their purpose is always safe and good. If you do have objective clairvoyant ability, all the exercises in this book will gently and safely help you develop and work with it.

Auric Sight

Auric sight isn't strictly clairvoyance, although if you take the term literally you have to agree that the ability to see auras is certainly a form of clear vision.

Auric sight is the ability to see the subtle energetic field or aura that emanates from all physical things. Everything, both living and nonliving, has an aura. Whatever you can think of has its own energy field that can be seen, felt, and observed. Even your favorite chair has an aura.

An aura can look like a photographic double image or a cocoon around a person, life form, or object. It can vary in texture, quality, and color. Let's try a few aura exercises to get things moving.

Exercise: Auras
This exercise will help you picture auras.

- Close your eyes and imagine that you see an aura around everything easily. Start with yourself. What does your aura look like at the moment? How big is it? What color is it?
- Open your eyes and look at an object close to you. Close your eyes again and imagine its aura. What does it look like and feel like? How is it different from your own?
- Finally, open your eyes and take a few moments to look more widely at your surroundings. Close your eyes again and imagine that everything around you has an aura. Trust your inner vision to give you interesting information. Focus in on particular people or objects and make a note of anything you imagine or receive.
- Complete the exercise by opening your eyes and taking a good look around. ▲

Developing auric sight often is simply a matter of learning how to refocus your eyes. Normally our eyes are focused on the physical nature of matter rather than the subtle energy fields around it. The next exercise will help you to do this.

Exercise: Refocusing Your Eyes
This exercise will help you refocus your eyes on the subtle energy fields that surround you. The soft light of evening is a good time to develop auric ability.

- Hold your hand about eighteen inches from your eyes. Look at your hand; notice the shapes, lines, and texture.

- Notice the outline of your fingers and thumb as you gently close your hand to make a fist and then release it again.
- Shift your attention from your hand to something in the distance, say a picture on the wall. Let your hand remain central but look through it to your object. Practice shifting your vision back and forth a few times.
- Notice how different your hand looks as you adjust your focus. Rest your eyes for a moment and then repeat the exercise, but this time leave your eyes focused on your distant object through or beyond your hand and notice what you see.
- You might just notice a small movement of light or energy around your hand or a double etched image. It doesn't matter if you don't see anything at first. Just rest your eyes and try again later.

Interpreting the Aura

Once you perfect seeing auras, you can begin interpreting them. How? You can interpret auras by thinking about the quality of the color you are seeing rather than a color itself. Is it clear and bright, or is it dull and muddy? Is the aura healthy and happy, or are you receiving several mixed signals?

We all interpret color differently, but it always helps to have a guide. The list of colors below is a good starting point. Use it as you practice seeing and interpreting auras.

The colors of an aura

Red: survival, fight or flight, strength, motivation, energy, power, anger, change

Orange: vitality, sexuality, exercise, pleasure, creativity, warmth, passion

Yellow: inspiration, power of the mind, study, ideas, cheerfulness

Green: nature, balance, harmony, calm, love, compassion

Blue: communication, healing, teaching ability, creativity, inspiration

Indigo blue: vision, intuition, psychic ability

Violet: wisdom, enlightenment, spiritual growth

Pink: love, warmth, tenderness, childhood, the impulse to nurture

Gold: love, brilliance, prosperity, creativity

White: purity, purification

Black: depression, crisis, restfulness, renewal

Nine

Clairaudience and Telepathy:

Tuning In to the Psychic Broadcast

Did you know that every day we have a stream of thoughts that provide us with a constant source of inner dialogue, impressions, judgments, and ideas? We do! Sure, it may be hard to hear it through the noise of our everyday lives, but it's there.

Psychic Spotlight

Much of our inner chatter is based upon beliefs and attitudes that we have formed already as a result of past experience. This helps us avoid making the same mistakes again and again.

By tapping into this stream of thoughts, you can improve your life and tackle problems in a new, enlightened way. Impossible, you say? Never! We *all* have the ability to access these enlightened thoughts, but some of us are more attuned to the frequencies they are broadcast on. Think of it as psychic tuning in! Depending on how you process information, it may be difficult, but the art of tuning in can be developed with practice.

Just like clairvoyance, clairaudience can be *objective* or *subjective*. Getting fuzzy on the meanings? Okay, here it is in a nutshell.

⁕ *Objective Clairaudience*

Have you ever heard your mom, dad, or a friend say something, only to turn around and realize the person wasn't there? That's *objective clairaudience.* You may hear sounds as if they are happening in the physical world. However, objective clairaudience is very rare—it can take time to develop.

⁕ *Subjective Clairaudience*

It's far more likely that you will receive messages through *subjective clairaudience.* The noises you hear are received internally as impressions of sound or words or thoughts, concepts and ideas that just seem to spring into your mind from nowhere.

Psychic Spotlight

Some people receive their best ideas from clairaudient messages. Solutions to problems and personal guidance may all be transmitted through clairaudience. You may even hear internal words of reassurance or sounds that brighten your mood.

Perhaps even more than any other psychic ability, clairaudience is a matter of tuning in to the right frequency. Psychic sound is said to vibrate at a particular rate, and the same is true for clairaudient sound. The key is to widen the range in which you are able to receive information through the hearing sense so that you can tell which sound comes from the psychic world.

Exercise: Tuning In

This exercise will help you get comfortable with tuning in to the right psychic frequency.

- Sit comfortably in your sacred space with your back supported and your body relaxed and open—don't cross your arms or legs. Breathe deeply and imagine a shield of golden light around your ears for healing and protection.
- Now imagine that the golden light is filled with a continuous chime that brings a sense of peace, happiness, and joy.
- Next imagine that you have a tuning knob like a radio, and you can tune your hearing to your own higher awareness. This is the part of you that sees the bigger picture of your life and can see what your purpose is.
- Ask that you work to serve the highest good, and imagine tuning your hearing to receive clairaudient information from your higher awareness. Sense a subtle sound change as you adjust your frequency.
- Note any information that comes to you through your inner hearing. You may receive very little at first, but keep trying. After a while you may find that your ears automatically tune in to receive clairaudient information when you focus.
- Complete the process by bringing your hearing safely back to normal and surrounding your ears with the protective golden light and sound.

When you have practiced tuning in a few times you may wish to listen for some specific guidance. Begin by taking a few minutes to write down some questions that are important to you and then tune in. Slowly ask your question and take time to breathe deeply and listen. Remember to make a note of any insights you receive and to protect your hearing once you are complete.

The Still, Small Voice Within

Imagine if you had someone who always knew what to do, always made the right choices for you, and knew all about you. Such a person does exist—it is you!

Within you is someone of great potential and great wisdom. Within you is someone who is growing and developing great magical abilities. Within you is your inner voice, sometimes called your higher self, inner guide, or creative spark. Most people keep their inner guide hidden away deep within themselves. But with every psychic development exercise that you do, your inner guide becomes stronger and more powerful in your daily life.

The following exercises will help you listen to your inner voice and meet your inner guide.

Listening to Your Inner Voice

This is easier than you think! The first step is to have confidence in your abilities, even if you don't think you have them yet! You can start doing this with two easy steps:

1. Seat yourself in a quiet place (your sacred space!), close your eyes, and enter a still state of mind.
2. Now put your concentration on the right, lower side of your head, to a point in the region of your inner ear. Now simply wait.

Now, you're probably thinking "this is silly." But don't give up yet. Clairaudient words of wisdom may just seem like common sense from a familiar inner voice, and indeed that is just what it is. We all receive a constant stream of information from our higher awareness, and a certain amount is clairaudient. We just need to remember to listen.

Psychic Spotlight

Do you sometimes hear names of people or things repeated over and over again for no reason? Do words, thoughts, and ideas keep coming to you from nowhere? The power of your own inner voice is closer than you think!

Andrew's Inner Voice

Here's what fifteen-year-old Andrew experienced when he listened to his inner voice:

> I usually bike home the same way each night, but for some reason I can't explain, something in my head told me to walk. It was a beautiful sunny day so I decided to walk by bike home. It took a lot longer than I thought, so halfway there I decided to hop on my bike. Something inside my head again said walk. I walked a little further and just as I was about to get on my bike I heard a cry of distress. It sounded like a cat, and sure enough hidden in a bush was a tiny, tiny kitten. I picked it up gently and put it in my basket and as I was walking down the road I saw a boy frantically putting up posters for—you guessed it—a lost kitten. I have never seen someone so happy when I handed the kitten over.

The more attention you give to your higher mind, the more likely you are to connect with it. Every time we listen to our intuition and act with integrity and honesty, we enhance our higher awareness. Your higher mind delights in supporting and helping you, so let it become your greatest ally. Consult that part of yourself when you need to make decisions. Take time to sit quietly and reflect.

Exercise: Connecting with Your Higher Awareness

Now it's time for you to make a connection. Give it a try!

- Sit comfortably with your back supported and your body relaxed. Breathe deeply, and as before, place a shield of golden light around your ears.

- Now imagine that your higher mind exists in a beautiful place of light and sound, and that the place is right above you. As you breathe, visualize a bridge leading to your higher mind and see yourself climbing to it.

- As you enter your higher mind you are surrounded by light, sound, and color. Take time to explore the feeling of this place and to listen to the sounds.

- You come to a full-length mirror. You realize that the image you see is the real you, the ideal you, the magical you—your inner guide. To your amazement your guide steps out of the mirror and stands in front of you saying, "I am the most creative part of you. I see that which you do not. How can I help you?" The voice is kind and gentle and loving.

- You sit down with your guide. You may request some insight or discuss a problem or ask what lies ahead for you in the coming week. You listen and remember what your guide has to say.

- Your guide tells you that he or she is always with you, and that as you spend more time together, he or she will become stronger and more of a blessing to you. Then your guide melts into you and you feel your true essence awakening. Your heart is filled with hope. You are greater than you imagine.

- When you leave, see yourself taking some of the images, sounds, and sensations with you back to inspire you in your day-to-day life.

- Walk back across the bridge, and as you do see yourself expressing your higher awareness in every waking moment. Gradually open your eyes and make note of any ideas or insights that have come to you. ▲

In time, all you will need to do is close your eyes and see, feel, or hear your inner guide and notice how your guide responds to situations. This will give you the clues you need as to what you should do and how you should respond to people and events around you. And the more you work with your inner guide, the more you will know that your psychic powers are coming to life within you.

Telepathy

Telepathy is another form of clairaudience. It is the ability to send and receive messages and information through the mind. With telepathy, there is no need for talking, no need for hand signals or facial expressions—it's all about the power of your mind.

Most of us are telepathic to some degree, but because telepathy is so often combined with body language cues we rarely notice it. You may have experienced telepathy if:

✳ You and your friend had the same thought at the same time.
✳ Before you pick up the phone, you know who is calling.
✳ You have felt someone's emotional or physical happiness or pain.

Telepathy is particularly common when you are very close to someone—like a best friend or boyfriend. Although most of us have experienced telepathy without knowing it, like any other psychic ability, it can be learned and strengthened through practice.

Strengthening Telepathic Connections

Telepathy works best if there are emotions involved. Emotions give thoughts a powerful boost. So if there is someone you feel really close to, why not practice with him or her first? Emotional closeness opens psychic channels. We often sense and feel things more easily with those we are close to. Is there someone you know who you feel is on the same wavelength as you?

Your human friends aren't the only beings who can help you communicate. Animals can have highly developed sensitivities as part of their survival instinct. Animals sense subtle changes in the environment around them and are extremely sensitive to emotions. If you have a pet, it can be a great assistant in your telepathic work. But to build a solid foundation for telepathic work with your pet, you need to spend a lot of time with it first and not try to force the connection. The stronger and happier the bond between you and your pet, the stronger the telepathic communication will be.

Telepathy works best if there is a genuine trust and feeling of safety between partners, whether they are animal or human. Below are some exercises and declarations for telepathic development that you might like to try as you discover this wonderful ability.

Exercise: Partnering Work

This exercise helps you learn to send and receive information. Just find a partner—a family member or a friend—and give it a try.

- Select a part of your partner's body as a target. Close your eyes and focus intensely on it.

- Imagine tickling it or pinching it for a few moments. Concentrate on feeling the sensation yourself before sending it to your partner.
- When you have finished sending information, open your eyes and compare notes about what your partner felt or thought about.
- Switch roles and let your partner target parts of your body. Concentrate on having fun while you practice. If you prefer, you could try projecting and receiving shapes instead. Visualize a square, circle, or triangle on the person's shirt sleeve.

If you keep practicing you might get a clearer sense of what you are best at: sending or receiving telepathic information.

Exercise: Sending Yourself a Message

This is a great exercise for teaching you how to send messages to your inner guide. Let it become your personal reminder for important events.

- When you go to bed at night, visualize yourself connecting to your inner guide.
- Decide on a time you wish to wake up in the morning, and visualize yourself waking up at that time rested and alert. (Hint: You may want to set your alarm, just in case!)
- Go to sleep.

If you wake up in the night take a look at your clock. Sometimes your inner guide gets a little stressed out, but after several times you should find that you wake within half an hour of the scheduled time.

Exercise: Sending Messages to Loved Ones

This exercise is as simple as sending good thoughts to the people you care about.

Although you may not believe it, long-distance telepathy can work. Why not give it a try?

Remember: Negative energy is detrimental to psychic development and will do harm to you rather than to the person you want to send your negative thoughts to! Thinking good thoughts is essential.

- Choose a person to whom you'd like to send good thoughts.
- Find a quiet, comfortable space and ask that your energy be sent.
- Now bring that person to mind and breathe deeply and slowly. As you inhale, see and feel healing light stream into you to heal and bless you. As you exhale, see that wonderful healing energy go from you to the other person to strengthen him or her.
- Do this for a few minutes. See and feel that person becoming strong. Offer a prayer of thanks for the healing, and then begin disconnecting, pulling your energy back.
- Bring the focus back to you, and take a moment to see yourself healed and strengthened by the process.

With this exercise you will be developing your healing skills for the benefit of others as well as yourself. The ability to heal is, we believe, a natural human gift, and just like psychic ability it can be stimulated and nurtured with practice, commitment, and a willingness to learn.

You Can Heal

A *healer* is a person who helps people feel better about themselves. Healing is much more than curing someone of an illness, though. Did you know that listening to a friend and being supportive when she is in crisis can be a healing act? Your friendship gives her a feeling of security and strength that encourages her to help herself.

Another type of healing is *hands-on healing*. This type of healing is used in many religious and spiritual traditions. It is sometimes referred to as faith healing.

You can be a healer whether you are religious or not. All you need are two very important things: a belief in the spiritual side of life and a positive, loving intention. The hands are simply used in the healing process to guide or direct the flow of healing energy. The healer may focus a greater amount of healing energy on a particular body part or toward an inner emotional state. Some healers report tingling sensations in their hands, while others report no change. Many recipients of healing talk enthusiastically about feelings of lightness, peace, release, or relaxation.

Your Healing Potential

Are you the kind of person who can't wait in line for a bus without someone telling you his or her life story? Natural healers unconsciously draw people to them who need help, advice, or just a sympathetic ear.

Helping to heal the world around you may be simpler than you think. Begin by paying attention to where help is needed. Once you start to really look at the people and things around you with an open mind, you'll be able to see the problems that people around you are experiencing. Perhaps one of your friends walks with her shoulders slumped as if carrying a heavy burden. She probably is. A teacher who looks tired and stressed is probably thinking about something that worries him greatly.

Eventually, you'll come to see that you are healing yourself just as much as you're healing others. That's because every moment of empathy you share with another helps you appreciate what you have and what you are.

Psychic Spotlight

When you really start to see what is going on in the world around you, don't be afraid to feel it. Accept that you have the gift of empathy. You don't always have to tell people anything or try to fix their problems; simply helping them feel understood may be all that is needed.

So without you realizing it, for example, when you listen to your best friend going through yet another relationship crisis, you may already be using your healing skills.

Barry's Buzz

Seventeen-year-old Barry had this to say about his psychic ability:

> I've always been a good listener and I get a buzz out of making people laugh, but I didn't realize that I had healing power until I had to be off school for a week. When I came back my teacher said that everyone had really missed me and the atmosphere just wasn't the same. It made me feel really good to know I was making a difference and developing my psychic ability just by being friendly.

Recognizing the healing abilities you already have is the first step toward developing new ones. When you acknowledge your healing potential, you encourage it to grow. People will be drawn to you because of who you are as a person as well as the healing energy that you give out.

Exercise: Healing Light

The exercise below will help you develop your healing skills.

- Sit comfortably with your back supported and breathe deeply. Now take your attention away from your body to a special peaceful place.
- Imagine that part of you can travel through space to a distant galaxy. In that galaxy is a beautiful star of golden light. This star contains an unlimited supply of energy that you can use for self-healing and for the healing of other people around you.
- Picture a beam of light being projected from the star through the depths of time and space and passing through your scalp and into your head.
- Every inward breath helps to draw the light into your body, and every outward breath helps to spread the light to every cell.
- The light stimulates and strengthens the love from your heart, and your heart becomes stronger and brighter. Now the light spreads down both your arms. Power is pulsating through you.

Repeat this exercise as often as you can to remind your body that you draw upon an infinite source of healing energy that exists around you in the universe.

Healing Help

When you start to direct healing energy to others, remember two very important things:

1. The healing energy you are giving comes from an inexhaustible supply—all you need to do is keep your thoughts positive and it will always be there.

2. The energy is coming from beyond you. You are a channel of healing light, not the source of energy yourself.

If you start to feel drained, this is a sure sign that you need to stop for a while and concentrate on self-healing. Practice imagining the energy that comes from outside of you. Prepare yourself for healing in a way that suits your beliefs. And finally, don't forget that whatever your beliefs, healing occurs best when you as the healer think good thoughts about yourself and others. Heal with love and respect, not with resentment and guilt.

Hints for Healing Yourself

Before you begin to practice healing on others, it's a good idea to try it out on yourself first:

* Begin with the meditation in the previous exercise, and then send healing light from your hands to your own body, heart, and mind.
* If you feel unwell, you might want to send the energy to the particular part of your body that is suffering.
* For example, if you have an infection, imagine the light passing from your hands into your immune system, releasing tension, discharging blocked energy, and awakening your body's natural healing wisdom.

Taking the Next Step

Now let's move on to healing an ailing plant before you try to heal another person. Here are some quick tips for plants:

* Have your hands near rather than on the plant in question.

Imagine its leaves, stems, flowers, and roots filling with healing light.

* Visualize the plant returning to full health. Don't forget, though, that you still need to take care of the plant physically as well as spiritually—continue to water, feed, and tend to it in the appropriate way.

Hints for Healing People

When healing people, so much depends on whether the person you want to send the healing to is a willing partner in the process. If the person is physically present:

* Encourage the person to sit opposite you. Then tell her to close her eyes, breathe deeply, and relax.
* Begin with your hands on or near the person's head.
* In your mind, connect to the source of healing light traveling to you and through you from the distant star. Imagine your heart filling with light. Picture that light flooding out of your body through your hands and into the head of the person.
* Imagine the color of the healing light changing until it reaches what seems to be the right shade for that person. Sense the light filling the head, brain, and face of the person, healing and balancing her.
* Picture the light dissolving fear, pain, and confusion and stimulating the body to heal. In your mind's eye, see that person happy and healthy.
* Now imagine all that healing light flooding to that person's heart and throughout and around her body, protecting, healing, and energizing her.

✳ Once you have done this, shake your hands to break the connection between you and your partner. Imagine this person now taken care of by her own self-healing abilities. Gently encourage the person to open her eyes.

If the person is not physically present, you can perform *absent healing*. You can do this through a combination of the power of thought and the power of love. Each thought you have is powerful and sends a subtle energetic charge through your body and out into the world at large. In essence, we are all engaged in telepathic communication whenever we think of someone. That person receives our thoughts even if she or he isn't aware of it.

To send absent healing:

✳ Breathe deeply and close your eyes. Take a few moments to think about the person you wish to send healing to.
✳ Silently ask this person's permission to heal him. If you don't know him personally, just think about his name or ponder the information you have about him.
✳ Now imagine this person surrounded by beautiful healing light. Sense that he is able to use that healing energy in whatever way is appropriate for his needs.

Psychic Spotlight

Tapping into the all-powerful source of love and spiritual healing can have many names, but most people in Western society call it prayer. So you could say that prayer is really psychic healing power—you become a means for directing or channeling positive energy to someone who needs to be healed.

We've covered a lot of ground in this chapter, so you may want to reread it or take a break for a while. You began to practice your clairaudient awareness and your telepathic ability, and you tuned in to your healing and creative powers. That was a lot of heavy stuff for you to take in. We'll keep things lighter in the next chapter. We'll let you float for a while. Come with us. It's time to investigate the world of spirit guides and helpers.

Ten

The Spirit World

Many psychics believe they are guided by spirits who can offer them valuable information. Sometimes these guides are people who are no longer living but who continue to offer guidance. You may find this talk about spirits scary or controversial or strange, but bear in mind that all we are referring to here is a kind of awareness that exists outside of your physical body, in the realm of thoughts and feelings. Sometimes these bundles of awareness may take spirit form. Psychics often talk of spirits who are more enlightened than most, such as monks, medicine men, shamans, mystics, or even angels. Let's explore this a little more.

Psychic Spotlight

Most of us have not one but a whole team of spirit guides who bring support to various aspects of our lives. True spirit guides always have your best interests at heart, and they will come to you only with love and warmth and concern for your development.

Working with Angels

Old legends tell of a group of angel spirit guides that watch over us when we are born and stay with us throughout our life. Working with angels is one of the safest ways to begin your work with the spirit realm. By opening to them first you can then have the angels protect you in all your psychic work. Earlier we learned how to create a sacred space and in the next exercise you will call on the four great archangels to bring protection to your sacred space and all your psychic development.

Archangel Tips

Here are some simple instructions for calling on the archangels.

Raphael

To call upon Raphael, face eastward. This archangel is associated with spring season, beauty, light, and healing.

* **Symbol:** The sun
* **Color:** Blue and gold
* **Gift:** Raphael is a bringer of miracles

Gabriel

To call upon Gabriel, face westward. This archangel is associated with winter, and is the bringer of love and hope.

* **Symbol:** Lily and white rose
* **Color:** White, black, and yellow
* **Gift:** Strength and protection

Michael

To call upon Michael, face south. This archangel is associated with autumn, strength, balance, and protection.

* **Symbol:** Flaming sword

* **Color:** Red
* **Gift:** Control, balance, and illumination

Auriel

To call upon Auriel, face north. This archangel is associated with summer, creativity, and abundance.

* **Symbol:** Fruit and green vines
* **Color:** Emerald green
* **Gift:** Opens us up to the blessings of Nature

Exercise: The Four Great Archangels

Enter your sacred space, or another place where you feel calm and comfortable. Practice saying the names of the four great archangels slowly and with three syllables each. Three is a creative and magical number, and each syllable gets equal emphasis.

Raphael: say Rahe fah ehl
Gabriel: say Gah bre ehl
Michael: say Me kah ehl
Auriel: say Ah ree ehl

Exercise: Magical Toning

Magical toning is a technique used all over the world to give power to prayer. Toning is the pronunciation of words with a special kind of breathing.

* As you inhale, say the archangel name silently. As you breathe out, say the name of the same archangel again. Practice until you feel comfortable, and then try to tone the following prayer. On the first line breathe in, on the next line breathe out, and so on.

Raphael in front of me
Gabriel behind me
Michael to the right of me
Auriel to the left of me
Angels surround, bless, and protect me ▲

You may find that this magical prayer is a really good way to begin
and end your psychic exercises. It will ensure that you are surrounded
and protected by loving spirits and that any spirits who make you feel
uncomfortable will be dismissed. With practice you will be able to
invite spirits and other guides into your life with great success. Don't
get discouraged if your spirit guides do not appear in ways that you can
easily detect at first. Remember, it's not the form but the information
you get that matters.

When you finish your psychic exercises, always thank your spirits.
Courtesy is as important when working with spirits as it is with human
beings. Not being able to detect your spirit guides doesn't mean they
aren't there. You simply may not be able to tune in effectively yet. All
energy begins with your thoughts, so even if you don't feel that your
guides are with you, imagine and believe that they are there. It opens
the bridge that will allow them into your life when the time is right.

Inviting Angels and Spirit Guides

Find a quiet, comfortable space and call to the archangels to protect
you. Now see a doorway opening before you, and step through it into a
sacred space. This could be a castle, a garden, a temple, or any place that
represents a sanctuary for you. Use your imagination and know that
in this place the spirit world and the human world can come together.
Now wait and see what spirits come to you. You may want to call one
of the archangels to come and visit you.

Visualize and imagine a large bubble of the angel's color drifting toward you. Out of this bubble the angel speaks out. If an angel comes to you, ask what its purpose is and if there is anything important that you need to know. Do not worry about answers. Do not worry that you are simply imagining it all. You would not be able to imagine it if there was not some reality to it. You may want to ask your spirit guide for some sign in the next week so you can verify its reality. When you are ready to leave, thank the guide. If it was an archangel, let it step back into the bubble of color and drift back to the spirit world. Breathe deeply and repeat your angelic prayer of protection. As you do, see and feel that you are returning to normal.

Loving Closure

One of the best things about working with spirits is the opportunity it gives to bring closure to the past. So often loved ones pass away before we get the chance to say all that we wanted. This makes healing difficult. Closure is simple but very powerful. If you want to speak to someone who has passed away, invite the angels to protect you. Then enter your inner sanctuary. Imagine what you would do and say if you could see this person again. Let your imagination run free. Take your time. When you are ready, say goodbye and thank you. Leave the place and return to normal, knowing that the past is healed and that this person can be with you whenever you allow.

Exercise: Meeting Your Guides

- Get comfortable and place a shield of golden light around your ears, as you did in the clairaudience exercises.
- Tune your hearing to the frequency of the higher mind, and imagine walking across the bridge to your higher mind.

- Once you're there, ask for contact with your higher guides. State that you are only open to guidance from sources that have your—and everyone else's—best interests at heart. Not all guides are trustworthy, but you're always safe if you ask them to help only if they serve the highest good.
- Imagine that your hearing, vision, and gut become attuned to the right frequency, so that you will become available to receive higher inspiration and support.
- Now visualize a small number of guides coming toward you and bathing you with feelings of love and acceptance. Notice what they look like, feel like, and sound like. Ask them for guidance. After you have listened to them, thank your guides and ask for their continuing support and protection.
- Gently take your attention away from your higher mind and your guides, and bring it back to the physical sensations of your body and the environment surrounding you. Make a note of any insights, ideas, images, or feelings you have received. ▲

As you try to get in touch with your guides, try not to think of your awareness as coming only from your mind or your body. Try to think of it as coming from the dimension of spirit. Scientific experiments can help you here. Carefully controlled experiments on animal learning patterns are beginning to prove the existence of intelligence outside the body and mind.

What About Ghosts?

No area of the psychic world gets as much attention as ghosts. Ghosts and spirits are often misunderstood. So forget everything that you have seen on television and in the movies. That includes headless bodies and strange floating beings. To benefit from what the spirit world has to offer, you have to let go of your fear. As long as you remember these three things, you have nothing to worry about:

1. The spirit world is not heaven or hell. There are as many different kinds of spirits as there are people. Think of the spirit world as a foreign country. It has its own customs and its own language. You can get the most benefit from visiting a foreign country if you take the time to learn the language and customs. That means the more you learn about the spirit world, the more comfortable you will feel.

2. You need to remember what we told you right at the beginning of this book—young people have natural psychic abilities. Most of the time, spirits can communicate more easily with you than with adults. You may have thought that the only way to communicate with spirits is by going into a trance, but there are far more effective and safe techniques for opening to the spirit world.

3. You control your contact with the spirit world—not the other way around. You are in charge. If you approach something that makes you feel uncomfortable, simply dismiss it and walk away. Almost all the problems with the spirit world arise when people think that spirits somehow have power over them. This simply isn't true. Dismiss spirits that make you feel anxious. Your true spirit guides are not going to make you feel uncomfortable.

Types of Spirits You May Encounter

There are many different kinds of spirit guides—some will be healing, some will be teaching, and some will be loving. However, these are the types that are most often spoken about.

Spirits

A *spirit* is any being that operates on a nonphysical level. It is a general term and can be used to refer to angels, guides, nature beings, and souls of those who have died.

Apparitions

An *apparition* is any object, being, or place that is supernatural. This word is often used interchangeably with the word *ghost*.

Ghosts

Ghost is a term applied to the visible spirit of a person who has died.

Angels

What is often called an angel may be nothing more than some kind of spirit guide who is assisting us. The word *angel* means "message." Therefore, any spirit being that brings a message is technically an angel. Often, though, the term is used to describe spirits that have not lived in human form but who embody a creative and loving intellect.

Disturbances

Disturbances are unusual experiences without any explanation. These can range from knocks and sounds in the night to people breaking out in chills in one part of the house. When you start awakening your psychic power, you will become more sensitive to disturbances going on around you. Sometimes they can simply be spirit guides trying to get your attention, but it isn't a good idea to invite disturbances. For example, it may seem like fun to play with a Ouija board or hold mock seances, but this kind of activity can be troublesome if you aren't sure what you are doing. It's like having someone crash a party; things can get out of control. This is what happens when you do things without proper training. You might get more than what you bargained for—a poltergeist, for example.

Poltergeists

Poltergeist literally means "noisy ghost," and refers to activities of spirits that are not just disturbing but distressful. It can be something as simple as unexplained noises in your house, or it can be as intense as things actually breaking. There has been a lot of debate as to the true nature of poltergeists. This kind of activity often occurs in homes where there are teenagers or children going through puberty, especially girls. One theory suggests that when you enter puberty a tremendous amount of psychic energy—corresponding to awakening sexual energies—is released in an uncontrolled manner, resulting in erratic expression of these energies. Don't worry, though. First of all, remember what we said about television and movies exaggerating things. Don't get carried away by your imagination! Second, you will never have to worry about things like poltergeists if you find creative outlets for your newfound psychic energy. Even though you are more attuned to the spirit realm than adults, you have a protective energy and a strong light surrounding you and will never experience anything like poltergeists if you stay healthy, balanced, and use your common sense.

Nature Spirits

Nature spirits are those beings associated specifically with nature. Every society once taught that there were spirits associated with anything growing upon the planet, and every tradition had its own way of naming them. In the Western world these nature spirits are often referred to as fairies, but they do have other names. Nature spirits are Mother Earth's children. They are as many-sided as nature itself and come in a great number of sizes, forms, and degrees of development.

Every flower has its fairy; every tree has its spirit. There are unicorns and other fantastic creatures within the natural world too. You may have had contact with this realm without even knowing it. If you ever walked past a tree and caught its fragrance, you received a greeting from its spirit. Nature spirits have magical abilities and can teach us much. They hold the keys to the mysteries of the natural world. Nature spirits are drawn to anyone who expresses joy at doing something, even if they aren't all that good at it. They also love music and have a natural affinity with those who love, appreciate, and protect all things in nature.

Spirit Animals

Many traditions taught that animals reflect our spirit. Animals that repeatedly appear in our dreams and in our lives can serve as messengers. They are referred to as spirit guides. Sometimes a spirit guide will show itself as an animal during our meditation. By studying that animal we can understand the role of that spirit guide in our life. To begin identifying your animal guides, answer these questions:

- Do you dream of certain animals regularly?
- Have you had unusual experiences with animals?
- Are there certain animals you are always drawn to?
- Are there certain animals you don't like?
- If you were an animal, which one would you be?

Psychic Spotlight

A spirit guide is any spirit that guides and protects us. It can take on many forms—a favorite relative watching us, or an animal he or she may choose to use to communicate to us through our clairsentient (feeling, selling, tasting), clairvoyant (seeing), and clairaudient (hearing) senses.

163

When working with spirit guides, always remember that it is not the form or appearance of your spirit guide that is important. What matters is the message that comes through. What does your spirit guide want you to know? Also remember that spirit guides will always help us but not *do* for us—the doing is your job.

Eleven

The Art of Divination

Now that you are more sure of your psychic abilities and are working to develop them further, it is time to explore the art of divination. Here are a few of the many tools you can use for divination. We've already talked about some of them; we'll get to the others in this chapter.

* Dream interpretation
* Reading Tarot cards
* Cloud watching
* Color reading
* Gazing into a crystal ball
* Tea leaf reading

Throughout time, people have tried to divine or know the future. Individuals who use divination are sometimes called psychics, soothsayers, sensitives, or intuitives, to name but a few of the terms used. There are many forms and types of divination, and we'll explore some here. Everyone is different, and you will find some forms of psychic expression easier to handle than others.

Your inner guide talks to you through whatever form of psychic communication is easiest for you to understand. Some of you will dream about things. Others will see auras or read Tarot cards. There also are divination tools that help you communicate with your inner guide. Some of the best known are numerology, astrology, and pendulums, but there are lots of others. All of these tools are fun and easy to use. They can help you better understand what is going on in your life and help you solve problems and be more creative. Each time you use these tools, your connection to your inner guide will grow stronger and you will increase your psychic power.

Psychic Spotlight
Divination, often defined as fortunetelling, means receiving knowledge about the present and future as if it is coming from a higher source.

Understanding the Future

You create possible futures by what you do or don't do in your life. For example, you are more likely to pass an exam if you study and prepare for it than if you don't. You create possibilities by your choices and actions in the present.

So in a way, you can know your future by learning to recognize future possibilities. You can begin to see what is likely in your life if you continue as you have been, and what is likely if you make a change. The key to seeing these patterns and changing them is to establish a strong connection with your intuition. The best way to do this is by working through the exercises in this book.

To understand how divination is possible you must understand two basic rules:

1. **All things are connected.** Every action has a reaction. Everything you do and think sets energy into motion and shapes your future. The trick is figuring out how things relate and how one act leads to another.

2. **All things are possible.** All things are possible, but some things are more possible than others.

Your psychic perceptions are usually probable patterns that are likely to occur, and your inner guide helps you see what is more probable than others. Remember, you always have free will. Fate is never fixed, and psychic work never takes away your ability to choose. There will always be things we don't know about, but you can use your psychic ability to discern probable outcomes and make changes that will make these outcomes more favorable to you.

Tools of Divination

An important part of developing psychic power is learning to use divination tools. These tools are bridges to your inner guide, providing you with wisdom, understanding, and insight. It might help to think of them as a kind of modem that gives you greater access to information and knowledge on the web of your psychic powers.

When you are just beginning to develop psychic power, divination tools can be really helpful. They give you something concrete to work with—a framework to help you test your intuition.

In time you won't need to use these tools because you will have established a strong connection with your psychic power and can draw on it anytime, anywhere. Until then you may want to explore and learn to use several tools, finding which ones work best for you in understanding and interpreting messages from your higher self.

Divination Tools

There are many types of divination tools to help you tap into the psychic part of yourself:

- Astrology studies the stars and planets to see how their movements affect your life.
- Tarot cards use symbols to help you interpret and understand events in your life.
- Numerology uses the idea that everything is based on mathematics. By interpreting the numbers in names and birthdates, life paths and potentials can be revealed.
- Dreams use images and scenarios to communicate messages.
- Pendulums and divining rods bridge the outer life of electrical impulses to the inner self. Interpreting the movement of the pendulum or rods gives answers to questions.
- Bibliomancy involves thinking about a particular problem or question and then randomly taking a book off a bookshelf and opening it to any page. Most of the time the page you turn to has an answer or some form of guidance for you.

As we have seen throughout this book, your inner guide usually communicates through symbols, sensations, and images. Your task is to figure out what these feelings, images, and symbols mean. We hope that the information given earlier in the book about clairsentience, clairvoyance, and clairaudience will help you in this communication.

And don't forget that all symbols and images can be personal, having a unique meaning to you. For example, an apple may be a sign of good health to many people, but if someone threw an apple at you when you were a child, it may represent attack. Your inner guide knows this and will use your personal associations if it presents the image of an apple to you. So always begin with what that image means to you. Ask yourself simple questions. How do you feel when you think of this thing? How does that fit in with your life now?

Trust your first impressions and think about them first before you consider other possibilities. How would other people or other books interpret these symbols? What do they mean to other people? Keep track of your images. You might want to write them down in your psychic journal. In this way you'll develop your own dictionary of symbols that you can use in addition to the A to Z glossary of symbols at the back of this book.

Cloud Watching

Remember lying back in the grass and looking up at the clouds? How many different things can you see in clouds? Clouds can take on many formations, and your inner wisdom can help you see images that answer your questions.

Psychic Spotlight

Cloud reading is one of the oldest forms of divination. It was commonly practiced by the Celts and Druids, who determined fortunes by looking at the formations and movements of clouds.

Why not go outside and let your imagination try to make sense of the shapes? Imagine that energy is growing within you, helping to stimulate your psychic vision. Don't stare intently at the clouds, just look at them softly—the kind of gaze you would have if you were daydreaming. Stay relaxed, and as you look at the clouds watch the shapes that appear. What you see can be quite revealing. It might be a good idea to think first about a question and then stare at the clouds.

Trust your imagination and your inner guide to help you see what applies to your question. Remember, you will see and feel what your inner guide knows you can relate to. With every cloud divination you will strengthen your ability to work with your inner guide and develop your psychic power. By developing this technique you have a tool that you can use anywhere as long as there are clouds.

Floating on a Cloud

You can look to the clouds to solve a question or problem by using your inner guide.

- Relax and quiet yourself and take a few moments to think about nature.
- Close your eyes and think about a question or problem.
- As you look at the clouds, pay attention to the formation. Your inner guide will help you recognize images that relate to your particular issue.
- When a cloud formation catches your eye, ask yourself, What does that image mean to me? Is it positive or negative? Notice any emotions that come up when you see an image.

Color Reading

Color reading is a divination tool you can use anytime, anywhere! Your inner guide will often use color when it is trying to communicate with you.

Psychic Spotlight

Many believe we subconsciously choose colors that we think will help us throughout the day. Your inner guide directs you to these colors. You've probably noticed that the clothes you set out the night before often don't feel right the next day. That's because you have had time to rest and reflect since you set them out. In psychic work you can divine the moods of others by the colors they wear.

Colors express energy and they can enter into many forms of psychic work. Each color has its own unique quality, as the information in the "colors" entry in the A to Z glossary at the back of this book explains.

Sometimes people choose to wear or surround themselves with a color that's opposite to how they feel or what they're doing to balance something about themselves. For example, academics tend to be drawn to blue to balance all that thinking.

Begin to get into the habit of looking at colors as a reflection of a person's mood or character. For example, look at others on the school bus and ask yourself these questions:

* What color is he or she wearing?
* Is the color revealing the person's character, or is it a balancing color? Trust your impressions on this.

In time you will be able to recognize basic qualities and moods in people by the colors they wear. You then will have insight into other people no matter how they present themselves. You also will be able to start choosing colors that can help strengthen and balance you. For example, if you need to be calm, wear blue; if you need to be energetic, wear red, and so on.

Crystal Gazing and Scrying

The crystal ball is the classic and best-known method of divination. We all have seen images of a carnival "gypsy" woman gazing into a crystal ball. Most people assume that the crystal ball itself has the power, but this isn't so. The secret is not the ball—it's the technique of *scrying*.

Scrying is an inner mental process, much like cloud watching. The big difference, though, is that when you scry you don't need to find shapes—you just see things.

Psychic Spotlight

Traditionally, a crystal ball is used in scrying, but you don't have to use a piece of crystal. Some psychics can scry on any surface they choose, such as a mirror, a bowl of water, or even their fingernails.

When you begin scrying, you might want to use one of these two simple items:

1. A bowl of water
2. A quartz crystal

Quartz crystals emit a form of electrical energy that helps to stimulate psychic powers, and water has a magical and mystical power of its own. You can find quartz in any New Age store. We recommend you find one that can fit into the palm of your hand. It doesn't matter what shape it is or how marked it is.

Trying at Scrying

Here's a simple scrying exercise for you to try:

- Begin slow, rhythmic breathing.
- Place your hands around the crystal or bowl of water. Focus on what the problem is, or on what you wish to know about.
- As you hold or touch the crystal or bowl of water, feel it coming to life. Imagine that energy is growing within you, helping to stimulate the psychic vision.
- Stay relaxed. As you look at the crystal or water, pay attention to its formations—watch how the light catches or reflects.

Your inner guide will help you to recognize images that relate to your question. Don't stare too hard at your crystal or bowl—just look softly.

Ask what these images mean to you. Pay attention to the emotions you feel. Remember, you will see and feel what your inner guide knows you can relate to and understand.

With every attempt at scrying you strengthen your ability to work with your inner guide. You increase the development of psychic power. In time the images you see will shift and become clearer. You will see clouds appearing and disappearing, and you may even start to see detailed scenes leading to great psychic vision for the future.

Tea Leaf Reading

Here's another fortunetelling technique that is fun and easy to try.

For tea leaf reading, it's best to make a cup of tea from loose tea leaves. If you don't have loose tea, don't worry. Just tear open a bag of tea and use the leaves from the teabag. Don't strain it. Drink almost all of it, leaving only the dregs (just a little bit of tea along with the leaves). Swish the dregs around in the bottom of the cup. Then turn the cup over, place the lip upward in the saucer, and let the dregs drain out. Pick up the cup and look at the patterns the leaves make as they stick to the inside. Now, here's what you do:

* As you look at the tea leaves you must want some picture or object to form out of the patterns. (You might feel quite alone at this point because you are closing yourself off to what is going on around you, and focusing on the tea leaves.)
* Feel as if your eyes are looking up, but let them stare gently downward at the leaves. Don't gaze rigidly.
* Does an object come to mind in the dark patterns of the leaves? What thoughts and ideas come to mind?

Get used to allowing thoughts to pop into your mind, even when you have no idea where those thoughts are going to end up.

Reading for Friends and Family

As you learn to use divination tools and as your psychic ability grows stronger, you may find that friends and family will take interest—they'll want you to do readings for them.

Divination Education

As you use divination tools, you may find that they stimulate your psychic development. Here's what happened to nineteen-year-old Lisa: "Sometimes I get impressions or insights when I see or touch my friends. Should I tell them?" How much should you tell someone when you pick up psychic impressions? It's hard to decide. Use your best judgment. Remember that interpreting impressions can be tricky. As a psychic you have great responsibility, and it is easy to hurt someone else with misinformation. If you are at all unsure, just keep quiet.

When you begin to read for others, let them know you are just learning and ask for their help and support. As you become more confident, you will find that you have to refer less to your notes and can rely more on your intuition. Just remember, though, to be as positive, constructive, and helpful as possible. And always trust your intuition.

Here are some rules for you to remember when doing readings:

* Always be supportive and encouraging.
* Let those you are reading for know that they always have choices. Help them work toward positive choices.

✳ If you do see challenges ahead for other people, encourage them to stay strong and make positive choices. Never, ever, *ever* tell them that something terrible is going to happen!

Fortunetelling of that kind is a million miles away from the joy and expectation and truth of true psychic work. No one can be absolutely sure of the future, but you can support people to make the best of their current choices and opportunities so that their future is as happy and as healthy as possible.

Psychic Checklist

Here are some other helpful things to remember as you do readings:

- If you do a reading for someone else, you take on a big responsibility. Don't abuse it. Never present information as the absolute truth or suggest that there is no room for choice. Divination tools give *one way* of looking at problems. They don't have all the answers.

- You are not a doctor, lawyer, psychiatrist, or teacher. If the person you are reading for wants guidance about health, legal, financial, or academic issues, encourage him or her to talk to an appropriate specialist.

- If someone is in danger, get help. If you believe that someone is in danger of harming himself or herself or another person, report the situation to that person's family or the proper authorities as soon as possible.

- Don't get out of your depth. If you aren't comfortable discussing certain areas of a person's life, tell her so.

- Be diplomatic. Be motivated by love and compassion. You don't want to alarm or panic anyone. Sometimes you have to say

> something that a person may not like to hear. Be very careful with the way you word things. Never say, "This will definitely happen." Say something more gentle, like, "I feel that you might be heading for burnout. What do you think about that?"

There will be times when you will stumble and find yourself reaching for words. Don't be frightened about saying the first thing that comes to mind. Psychic readings rely on your first impressions. If you are worried about what to say next, or if you are rehearsing what you are going to say, it is not working. Psychic work is all about going with the flow. Nothing should feel forced or difficult. Most of us are lucky enough to be able to walk without thinking about it. That's what you have to aim for with your readings. You get so familiar with connecting to your inner guide that you can talk without effort.

Above all, remember to be positive and upbeat. This advice applies to readings you do for yourself as well. Everything that can happen has a range of negative and positive possibilities, and you, as a reader, have a duty to stress the positive. You can mention the negative, but let the person you're reading for know that positive choices can be made. We find that the word *but* can be very useful. For example, if you sense that the person you are reading for is hurt and upset, say something like, "There may be pain and heartache now, *but* you will be able to learn from the experience and find something better to replace what you have lost." Also, if the person asks you to help her make an important decision—for example, Should I leave him or stay?—remember that your task is not to tell her what to do. You must only help her explore the pros and cons of each choice and then allow her to search within her heart for the best possible solution.

One last point: Always finish your reading on an optimistic note and with good news. Do what you can to return the person you are reading for to the everyday world on a high note. So make a joke, sing a song, or break open a bottle of your favorite drink.

The Greatest Good

As you work toward psychic development and begin to use your healing powers for the benefit of others, it is good to know that you live in an age when cultures are beginning once more to work with psychics and healers. Psychics are working with doctors, scientists, law enforcement agencies, and business associates. If you handle your unique psychic potential with love and with positive intention for your own greatest good and the good of all concerned, your abilities will blossom. Your psychic potential will stimulate your self-growth and have a positive effect on all areas of your life and your relationships.

Twelve

Using Psychic Ability in Your Daily Life

Psychic power can be a fantastic thing, giving you glimpses of the future to help you make choices in life and alert you to things that may not be what they seem. But don't think that psychic power is going to make your life an easy ride and solve all your problems. Developing psychically will help you see that the world really is a place of endless opportunities and that you really have within you tremendous potential. Using psychic power can help bring many wonderful benefits to all aspects of your life. Even when you don't understand psychic information that comes to you, you should accept it and trust it. That information can help you in every area of your life, from school to dating, family, friends, and more.

Psychic Spotlight

Never forget that you are always the one in control of your psychic development. You are the one who makes your choices!

School

Because psychic ability is often seen as an aspect of our spiritual side, many people assume that it just doesn't blend with school and work. Nothing could be further from the truth.

Developing your intuition can help you work smarter. You'll be more in tune with what it takes to pass your exams, get good grades, or stay in your teachers' good graces. You also can use your psychic ability to help you make decisions about career paths that you might want to follow when you leave school. If you aren't sure what you want to do with your life, your intuition might help you get in touch with the right career choice for you. If you know what you want to do, your intuition can guide you in the right direction and make your efforts to get where you want more fruitful.

Psychic Spotlight

School is a huge part of your life, so why not use every tool available— including your psychic power—to make your efforts as positive and as productive as possible?

If you're doing a reading for someone else from your school . . . don't lie! Remember what an important role you are playing for them. If you see that someone is having difficulty with a school assignment, you can say so, but remember that your words will have great impact. Sometimes failing an assignment can be a wonderful learning experience, because it helps us find out what we need to do to succeed next time. You will never find a safer environment than school, where you can fail with so few consequences. Encourage the people you read for to enjoy what they are doing at school and to try as many things as they can, even if they are afraid of failing.

Exercise: Alternate Nostril Breathing

This yoga breathing exercise is a wonderful quick fix when your energy drops or you feel drained throughout your school day. Nostril breathing energizes our whole system, whereas mouth breathing makes us susceptible to health problems. With this technique you breathe alternately through each nostril, inhaling through one nostril, holding your breath, and then exhaling through the other one. The effects of this exercise will improve memory and help you study more effectively.

- Begin with a slow exhale and, using your thumb, close your right nostril. Inhale slowly through your left nostril for a count of four.
- Keeping the right nostril closed, use your fingers to close down the left nostril so both nostrils are closed for a count of four.
- Keep your left nostril closed, remove your thumb from your right nostril, and exhale for a count of four.
- Then switch nostrils, closing down the left nostril and inhaling through the right nostril for a count of four.
- Repeat four or five times, and then perform the grounding techniques you learned earlier in this book.

Career

Your career can provide you with the stability you need in life. You can pay your way and take charge of your life in a way you were not able to before, and you get recognition for doing it. That's why it is important that you have career aspirations and goals and strive for things. Just remember, though, that there is a fine line between chasing after something and letting your whole world revolve around it. Always keep your goals in mind, but never sacrifice your happiness.

What Are Principles?

Principles are things like honesty, love, discipline, loyalty, and integrity. There are lots of others, and your heart will easily recognize them. To grasp why a life that isn't based on them won't work, think of a life based on their opposites: dishonesty, hatred, indulgence, betrayal, immorality, and so on. In this book you may have already noticed that all the exercises are based upon one or more principles. That is where their power and magic come from.

Creating Wealth

Contrary to popular belief, wealth isn't about money. It is about feeling happy and fulfilled. Money is important—there is no denying that—but it is far more helpful to figure out what "wealth" means to you. What do you want in life that you think money will get you? What will make you happy? By now, you know that you can use your psychic abilities to discover what will make you happy.

You can envision your wealth and your future by planning for them now. Buy a scrapbook and start collecting pictures of things you want to do, the kinds of people you'd like to meet, and places you'd like to go. Create a sensory experience of your goals. Look at your scrapbook every day and imagine what it would be like living your dreams. See what you'll see, hear, and feel. Do this as often as you can every day. This is the way you prepare yourself to receive the good things life has to offer.

Love, Sex, and Dating

Let's face it—these are the subjects that are on your mind most of the time. If you've started reading for your friends, you know that many of the questions they ask are about love—where to find it and how to keep it; whether or not they'll ever have a boyfriend; and will it last forever? Well, you can't always predict the future, but you can do the exercise below to find out what kind of person would be your ideal date.

Exercise: Who Is Your Ideal Date?

- Grab a pen and paper.
- Visualize exactly what kind of person would be perfect for you, and write it down in great detail. What does he look like? What does he sound like? What are his interests?

- See this person coming into your life.
- Ask your inner guide for guidance to help you find that perfect mate.
- Thank your inner guide, and then return to your daily life secure in the knowledge that one day you will meet the guy (or girl) of your dreams.

Sara's Story

Here's what fourteen-year-old Sara had to say about her experience:

I did a visualization exercise a few months ago to meet someone. In the past I've only thought about having a boyfriend, but I wasn't specific. This time I was. Nothing happened for four months, and then it worked. I've met someone who is right for me. And I helped two of my friends last week. I knew they liked each other but were too scared to make a move, so I imagined them holding hands. Believe it or not, they got together a few days later.

Now, don't get upset if you don't meet someone after doing this exercise. It doesn't mean you'll end up alone! Your inner guide may be trying to tell you that now isn't the best time for love, and that it might be good to put your energies into other things.

This doesn't mean you shouldn't ever date or ask your inner guide about your close relationships. Of course you should. It just means that you should not get obsessed with or center your life on someone else. The same applies to sex. Whether you are in a relationship or not, the issue of sex is always there. Should you or shouldn't you? Nobody can make that decision for you, but try to remember that having sex will not make you feel adult. If you only learn one thing from your psychic work, we hope it is this: The only person or thing that can change your life or make you feel better about yourself is you!

Family

The teenage years tend to be the time of maximum conflict with parents, authority figures, or adults in general. They want one thing, and you want something else. They want you to do what they think is right, and you want to do what you think is right. Neither party seems to understand the other. You may sometimes feel as though your parents come from another planet and that you get no respect. So how can psychic work help you?

Psychic Spotlight

If you don't like the way your parents are treating you, if you don't like the situation at home, if you hate your brothers and sisters—the answer isn't to rebel, come home late, or run away to get them to see your point of view. The answer is to change the way you behave. And your intuition is great at suggesting ways you can do this.

The way you respond to your parents influences the reaction you get from them. For example, suppose that you want to talk to your mom and she half ignores you because she is busy paying the bills. If you then walk away, you have taught her that if she ignores you, you will leave. If you yell and scream at your parents, you have taught them that you are childlike and irresponsible. If you are willing, however, to listen to other people's points of view and stand up for yourself, you'll demonstrate that you are mature and responsible, and you'll soon find that adults will start to take you seriously.

Be Safe and Sane

If you feel trapped or in danger and can't get anyone to listen to you, confide in an adult you trust. Take care of yourself. You are worth it. Here are some phone numbers that might help:

Rape, abuse, and incest: 1-800-656-4673

Neglect: 1-800-422-4453

Violence: 1-800-799-7233

Suicide: 1-888-793-4357

Although your parents can be a great source of strength and love and you should respect and love them, make sure you are being true to yourself. Care about what your parents think and feel, but remember that ultimately *you* are responsible for your life and your actions. Psychic work is all about staying centered and balanced and not being pulled in directions by other people or things. Make sure you please yourself as well as other people.

Friends and Relationships

No doubt your friends are probably soooo important to you. What are your relationships with your friends like? Has your psychic work throughout this book helped you understand your friendships better? Has it helped you understand yourself better?

The most important relationship you have is the one that sets the tone for all the other relationships in your life: the relationship you have with yourself. Everyone in your life will watch how you treat yourself, what you expect of yourself, and whether you can stand up for yourself. If you treat yourself with respect, you signal to others that you are a person who is to be treated with respect.

Psychic Spotlight

Developing your psychic gifts is all about helping you understand who you are and what you want from your life. In life you always get what you give. How can other people give you what you won't give yourself?

Take a moment right now to think about the types of relationships you are in, whether they are romantic, friendly, family, work, or something else. How can your intuition help you improve on these? Often it works by helping you gain insight into the other person's way of thinking so that you can understand him or her better and get a sense of what motivates him or her.

Once you know where another person is coming from, you can make great strides to connect and communicate with him or her. Your intuition also keeps you in touch with your own needs and what you can do to help yourself in relationships. For example: You form a great new friendship, but a year or so later you start to argue and dislike each other. If you really think about it, you might remember that when you met the person, your inner voice warned you to stay away. Why not refer back to the people-reading and "exploring someone" exercises in Chapter 6 to help you avoid such problems in the future?

Despite hearing these inner alarms, many people choose to ignore their intuition. Often they are afraid to trust their own judgment because they have made mistakes in the past. Once you have tuned in to your intuition it can act both as a warning signal and a confirmation that your own judgment is right on.

Many intuitive people believe that each person you come into contact with is there to teach you something very specific. For example, your parents are teaching you discipline, and you are teaching them patience. Even a disloyal friend can teach you something, whether it's the importance of loyalty or the necessity of ignoring nastiness. But if you are not sure what to think of someone, take your time, get to know him or her, and trust your intuition.

Appearance

Psychic study is all about finding the inner person and being positive and hopeful about your life. It's a cliché, and you have probably heard it time and time and time again, but it's true: It is what's inside that counts. No matter how hard you try, you won't look good on the outside if you feel lousy on the inside. So before you start comparing yourself to your friends, please remember that you don't have to have a certain amount of money or look a certain way to be happy.

A major part of feeling good on the inside is learning how to take care of yourself. Once again, psychic work will remind you of the principle of balance. You need to learn to relax and take time to treat yourself to some tender loving care. How? Use your common sense: Eat healthy food; get enough sleep; exercise regularly; say no to drugs, smoking, and alcohol; use your brain; surround yourself with those who care about you; and find some interest or hobby that inspires you. Basically, lead a balanced, healthy life.

Health

Most doctors agree that the mind has a profound effect on our well-being. We are not saying that all health lies within you, but you can use your psychic power to become healthier.

As studies on cancer patients have shown, imagination and visualization can improve your health. They are not a substitute for medication that you need to take, but they can be used in combination with treatments prescribed by your doctor. You also can use imagination and visualization to boost your immune system to protect you against illness.

Exercise: Think Yourself Well
Do you remember the healing methods that you learned in Chapter 9? This exercise will help you put them to use.

- The next time you get a cold, headache, stomachache, or just feel generally unwell, close your eyes and imagine that your immune system is made up of lots of little pale-colored jellyfish creatures.
- See the creatures as strong and purposeful. Now imagine traveling inside your body to the area that needs healing, and notice what you see. You might see an infection, or lots of tiny black cells. Now the jellyfish are going to destroy those black cells.
- When the black cells have gone, imagine the jellyfish happily swimming off and patrolling your bloodstream. Now imagine a healthier you sitting in front of you. See how the person looks, smiles, and so on. Now step into the healthier you and enjoy how much better you feel. ▲

The single biggest cause of ill health among teens is stress. We all need a certain amount of positive stress, as it actually motivates us to do things like get out of the way of an oncoming vehicle or do well on an exam. However, it is continual, negative stress that is dangerous. If you are continually pumping stress hormones around your body because you feel tense after an argument with your parents, or dislike a teacher or your school, or are worried about your boyfriend or girlfriend leaving you, you are putting an unnecessary strain on your body. A big stress factor is negative thinking, which we explored in Chapter 4. Continual worry and anxiety eventually will cause bad moods, mistakes, and even poor health. This happens because your natural defense mechanism is being triggered too often by negative stress.

Here are some simple psychic techniques you can use to diminish stress.

* If you sometimes find yourself daydreaming or feeling relaxed, don't fight it. Go with the feeling, and give yourself ten minutes to unwind.
* Ask yourself these questions every day:
  * Who or what in my life makes me feel happy?
  * Who or what in my life makes me feel loved?
  * Who or what in my life makes me feel passionate?
  * Who or what in my life makes me feel strong?

* Imagine and create a vivid picture of what makes you feel good. Do this every day when you first wake up, and you will find that it has a powerful effect. Instead of feeling down when you wake up, you will begin each day feeling happy.
* Try physical exercise. Swimming, running, or any other exercise that oxygenates the blood makes controlling stress easier. Of course, you also know all the usual things. Don't smoke, drink alcohol, or do drugs. Eat well-balanced meals. Good food is fresh food—plenty of veggies and grains. Drink plenty of water.

Why is visualization so effective for boosting health? Because when you use all of your five physical senses to visualize, you involve your emotions as well, and research has shown that emotions can interact with your body's systems. Try it now. Imagine a warm, sunny day with someone you love. Doesn't your body already feel warmer and more relaxed? Sensory images are the language of your body, and you can combine them with your psychic ability to help heal and improve both your body and your life.

Goals and Dreams

Do you know what you want out of life? If you do, congratulations! You have a clear goal to work toward. Just make sure it is a realistic goal. Think carefully about your motives. Are you basing them on your principles? If you aren't, then happiness will elude you.

But what if you aren't sure what motivates you, or what your hopes and dreams are, or whether what you think you want is really right for you? The exercise below can help you.

Exercise: Live Your Dreams

- Visualize a time in your life when you got something you really wanted. It could be a gift, an exam result, a ticket to a concert, or anything of your choosing.
- What were the factors that made you successful in getting this?
  - Did you work for it?
  - Did you ask for it?
  - Did you just hope?
- What were the obstacles that might have kept you from achieving this goal? Did anyone tell you not to do it?
- Did you have to overcome your fears?

- Now close your eyes and imagine your inner guide looking down on you. This being wants you to live your dreams. Ask this being what you should do to bring more of these qualities into your life.
- Ask your wise guide what you should do when you feel discouraged. ▲

Remember that your intuition always wants you to learn and grow. Keep in mind that you are still learning, and it may be a while before you feel inspired. Perhaps learning patience is a big part of your current lesson! Many factors may need to become clear before the path itself becomes clear.

Exercise: Coin Toss

If you're still feeling restless, there's something you can do to get answers about what you think, feel, dream, and imagine: Flip a coin!

- Think about the question that you need to ask. Form it in your mind as a yes-or-no question: Should I date so-and-so? Should I apply to law school? and so on.
- Take a coin and flip it. Heads is yes and tails is no. Okay, what was the answer?
- But wait! There is more to the exercise. Think about how you felt about the outcome. Were you disappointed, relieved, excited, or fearful?
- Admit it—did you immediately want to flip the coin two more times to get the best of three?

Every one of your responses is an example of your psychic self talking to you, and that's more informative than the heads or tails of a coin. All too often, we expect our intuition to be a booming voice saying "do this" or "don't do that." Your intuition is more likely to speak through subtle feelings, inner nudges, or physical sensations. Try to learn to pay attention to your inner guide.

Happiness

All of us have days when we feel depressed or don't have much energy. Did you know you can use your psychic powers to create happiness?

The first way your psychic training can help you was covered back in Chapter 4, where we discussed the power of concentration. Concentrating on the present moment or on a goal, task, or exercise, as we recommend in the book, helps you forget about all your worries and helps you get one step closer to happiness. Every time you concentrate, your unconscious mind takes note. Life then becomes easier and more effortless.

Just pause for a moment and think about what happiness really is for you. Some of you may think that happiness comes from the outside—from working hard, from making money—but that isn't the whole story. What is happiness like for you? Think about a time when you really felt great, or imagine what it would be like to feel happy. See what you saw, hear what you heard, and feel how good it feels. What you are doing here is teaching your mind to get your body to create the chemicals that lead to good feelings.

Psychic Spotlight

Happiness isn't something you can earn or buy; it is a state of mind. It is the response to what is happening in your life. The good news is that you can learn to have that response more often!

Quickie Endorphin Release

Endorphins are the feel-good hormones your body produces. They are released every time you laugh, love, and fully relax. Let's learn a technique to help you release those wonderful endorphins whenever you want to.

- Imagine a button in your mind with *endorphins* written on it. Or it could have a symbol like a smiley face or a flower on it. Imagine it now. In the future, you can just push that button any time you want or need an endorphin release.

- When you get the hang of this, just keep pressing that button through the day. You will eventually train yourself to feel good.

Hope

Let your psychic work remind you that however hard life gets, however much it hurts when you get dumped, flunk your exams, or lose your friends, you still have hope. You can always hope that you will change, that things will improve, that you will find an answer to your problems. The future is never fixed. The outcome of your story is not a certainty, but a possibility. You can always change the situation if you have the desire and the courage to take the necessary steps.

Psychic Spotlight

Never forget that you have within you all you need to succeed. You are the beginning and the end. You have the power and the magic within you. And developing your psychic power can help you find that power and magic.

Precautions and Protections

As we have seen, there are lots of benefits to psychic work. However, there are still three issues that you will always have to deal with as you work with your natural abilities. You will have to learn how to handle your sensitivity, how to face your fears, and how to believe in yourself. Now that you have started to awaken your psychic power, you need to pay attention to these three areas. Let's look at each in turn.

Handling Sensitivity

Developing your psychic gift is one part of the story. Learning how to turn it on and off so you don't become too sensitive is another part. Psychic development will increase your potential for empathetic responses to people and places around you. You may no longer be able to ignore things the way you used to do. You may see and feel things you don't want to.

Working with psychic power will make you more sensitive to everything going on around you. When you are empathetic, someone else's physical feelings, emotions, and attitudes can affect you so strongly that they almost feel like your own. For example, a friend fails her driving test and you feel her disappointment, or your brother breaks an arm and you feel pain in your own arm. When you develop your psychic ability, outside impressions register more strongly, and you are more likely to receive impressions of feelings and physical sensations that are not your own.

How Sensitive Are You?

- Are you easily persuaded by others to do things you normally wouldn't?
- Are you really shy?

- Do your moods change as you go from one group to another?
- Do you feel drained after being with people?
- Do you always seem to know what others are feeling?
- Are you touchy-feely?
- Do you get emotional at times, and take things more personally and seriously than others?
- Do you have a tendency to take on everyone else's problems?
- Do you love animals?

If you answered yes to more than two of the questions, you are a sensitive, empathetic person, and you will need to protect yourself.

For example, if you find it hard to disconnect from others, try visualizing a way to separate yourself from them. You might imagine that you're cutting a thread that's between you and the other person, or you might imagine going to a special room and closing the door. You may even need to disconnect from loved ones in this way. You will reconnect again, but if you are empathetic you may need to have some time every day when you are not linked to others so you can feel more objective and calm.

If you find yourself becoming too sensitive, visualize yourself as a king or queen who can see everything with balance and insight. Call upon the part of yourself that knows how to detach when feelings that you pick up from your environment get to be overwhelming.

Ana's Angst

Here's what thirteen-year-old Ana wants to know about psychic powers: "Can someone use psychic power against me?"

Don't buy into the rumors of psychic intrigue. It will block your development. If you keep yourself balanced and healthy, and focus on what you are doing and not what others are doing, you have nothing to fear.

Facing Fear

Fear is an essential part of life—it makes us alert and perceptive. Fear is only dangerous when you allow it to go beyond its function of alerting you to dangers and instead let it control your life. The only way to dispel fear is to bring it out in the open and face it. Once you can recognize fear, you often can let it go.

As you work within the psychic realm, you may find that you have to face some of your hidden fears. You may experience things you feel uncomfortable with. Questions and doubts will creep into your mind. When this happens, call upon the brave warrior inside you. Warriors are strong and determined to get things done, whatever the difficulties. They find ways to make things work and don't give up just because something is difficult. They only give up when something is foolish. If you find yourself feeling uncertain, visualize yourself as a warrior and say, "I am the warrior of my life." Respond to life with courage and responsibility.

Exercise: Wipe the Slate Clean

One of the easiest and most fun ways to dispel the problems in your life is to imagine just wiping them away as if cleaning off a classroom chalkboard.

- Imagine yourself standing before a large chalkboard.
- Take the chalk and draw out your problem or question.
- Visualize taking a step back from the chalkboard and taking a seat as your inner guide looks at your question.

- You watch as the answer starts to appear on the chalkboard, wiping away your problem or question. Trust what you feel here. Even if you can't actually see the answer in your mind, trust that the message has been sent telepathically to your inner guide.
- Thank your inner guide, and then imagine yourself leaving and feeling confident. Open your eyes. Within a week you should have the guidance that you need.

Believing in Yourself

Even though you are just working with your natural gifts, many people will think you are doing something out of the ordinary. They may not be very understanding of your work, and this may cause you to feel lost and isolated at times.

Lindsay's Lesson

Here's what fifteen-year-old Lindsay had to say about her psychic work:

I stopped working on my psychic exercises for a few months last year. Somehow my friends found out what I was doing and they started calling me psycho. It was really hurtful and I didn't want to be an outsider, so I just stopped. I realized how wrong it was for me to give up something I wanted to do in order to fit in when a boy called Paul in our class won a scholarship to a world-famous music college. Because of his musical gifts and obvious talent my friends used to call him a geek. I could see then that all that name-calling was really ignorant. Imagine if Paul had stopped studying music because he wanted to fit in—he would never have achieved his dreams.

At the other extreme, you may try to portray your power as something special—a gift that nobody else has. Beware: Statements about being special or different all reflect a low sense of self-esteem.

If you are feeling out of place or unbalanced as you develop your psychic power, draw once again upon the wisdom of the wise person in you. There will always be things in life we cannot control, and people we won't get along with, but the wise one will help us choose the best of our possibilities and opportunities. Developing your psychic power helps you tune in to this guidance more easily, allowing you to gain knowledge and understanding that will be the key to success in life. So call upon the wise one when you need to believe in yourself. Tell yourself that you are the wise one in your life and that you have great understanding and confidence.

Uncommon Sense

Remember, psychic experience isn't always enlightening and beneficial, and you need to find ways to sort out the good from the bad. Certain problems in life can be avoided by developing certain qualities, and the same is true for psychic work. Most of these recommendations are just common sense:

* Take care of your physical as well as your spiritual self. In short, eat well, exercise, and get fresh air.
* Try to develop greater self-belief.
* Don't be afraid to examine your feelings.

Ask lots of questions and keep an open mind. Don't blindly accept what you are told. Seek out answers and explanations.

Remember that no one else knows what is best for you. The future is never fixed. Your intuition can highlight possible futures for you. It can advise you, warn you of potential dangers, and encourage you to make better life choices, but it cannot make decisions for you. You and only you are the one who decides what is going to happen in your life.

When you are bold enough to follow your heart and your dreams, you uncover your sacred self. And that is when the magic begins.

The Incredible Journey

Developing your psychic power is a big adventure, an incredible journey that will last a lifetime. Ahead of you lie some exciting and wonderful experiences, as well as some that are strange and sad. Life doesn't always go in a straight l secret of happiness doesn't lie in getting what you want. The true art of living is found in how you react to the changing situations you find yourself in. Let your psychic power help you react with wonder, curiosity, wisdom, courage, determination, common sense, and, above all else, hope.

Wouldn't it be amazing if . . .

* You knew the wisest person in the world, the one who understood everything about you and your life?
* You could ask this person for guidance and advice at any time, and he or she could help you make the right choices and decisions?

This person does exist.

It's *you*.

Glossary

A to Z of Psychic Symbols and Images

The A to Z of psychic images and symbols that follows is presented simply to get you thinking along the right lines when trying to interpret messages from your inner guide. There is no such thing as a fixed and definite meaning for any symbol or image. Keep in mind that what the image or symbol suggests to you may be entirely different from what it suggests to someone else.

Do make sure that you pay great attention to the details of the image or symbol that you experience or dream about—the color, the size, the location, the people who are present, what role you play, how you feel, and so on. These are all vital clues to help you understand the message that is being sent to you by your inner guide.

In giving you these interpretations we are assuming that you will relate them to aspects of your own life, but you can use them to help you understand information that you sense about other people as well.

abduction:

This could be a sign that you will carry out your plans in spite of opposition and obstacles. It also could indicate that you are following the crowd rather than expressing your individuality. Your inner guide will know which of the above applies to you.

abyss:

Any hollow space can indicate challenges that lie ahead. It also may be a warning from your inner guide to make sure you don't spend more than you earn.

accident:

Accidents can imply carelessness, a need to be careful or watch out for mistakes. Do other people cause the accident? This could be a warning. The location will give clues as to where the problem is rooted—at home, school, or work. If you don't know the location, this could be a sign that things are out of control and you may feel that you can't cope.

acrobat:

Are you or someone you know bending over backward to please? Do you feel you are being forced into something? Are you waiting to be noticed? If you are doing a balancing act in your dream, do you feel as if you are living on the edge with some situation in your life?

acting:

A sign that in some situation you feel that you're playing a role instead of being genuine.

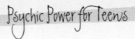

adrift:

Do you feel that you are drifting without direction? Trust your inner guide to show you a way to reach land safely.

alien:

Are you feeling misunderstood, or are you in a situation that you just don't understand? This also could be encouraging you to further explore the mysteries of life.

alleyway:

Alleyways or tunnels indicate how you view your life right now, and that speaks for itself. Is it dark and forbidding? Are you running, or walking, or sitting? Is there light at the end? Are you looking for a way out? Are you feeling trapped? Are you calling for help?

amusement arcade:

Are you winning and having fun, or losing and feeling disappointed? Again, this speaks for itself. Perhaps you need to think about your timing and decide whether you should keep going or quit.

angel:

Angels are messengers that bring special information for you. They also may bring reassurance and comfort. This image is extra special if it comes at a time when you feel really low. An angel is a symbol of love, joy, and peace, so to dream of one indicates success, happiness, and the answer that you are looking for.

animal:

Your basic instincts and reactions can be reflected in animals. If you were the animal in the dream, what did you feel? Do you recognize a particular strength? Perhaps this is something you need to develop. A lion, for example, represents bravery. An animal may also be a warning. For instance, a snake could mean that you need to be more wary of someone in your life. Sometimes your own pet is a sign of comfort and loyalty when you need reassurance.

athlete:

Your inner guide is telling you that you are a strong person, but you need to take care that you don't overstrain yourself.

baby:

Babies can symbolize new ideas or hidden potential. Do you see the baby, or is it handed to you? Giving birth can mean a new start. What are your feelings about the baby? If you feel anxious, perhaps you need to think things through.

bag:

If you are carrying heavy bags, what is your real-life burden? Is the bag yours or someone else's? Did you offload or dump the heavy bag? You may feel that your responsibilities are a bit heavy right now. Does something good or bad come out of the bag? Is your bag hiding something? Or are you going on a trip?

ball:

If you are playing ball with a team this may be about cooperating with others, so how well you are doing indicates how

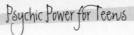

well you are doing in a group situation. Are you scoring goals? If you are, you feel great about yourself and your popularity. If you miss the goals, you could feel that you are letting the team down. Playing ball on your own perhaps indicates a need to do your own thing.

beach:

Do you long to get away from it all? If you are alone and all is peaceful, a new start may be on the horizon. If the sea is stormy, you may be feeling emotional. On the whole a beach is a sign of vitality and fun, and the message is that your creative talents are coming out and things are looking bright for you right now.

bear:

Is there someone you know who is grizzly or short-tempered? Or is it indicating someone cuddly? Perhaps you need a cuddle right now. Bears also can be magical, and when they appear they may be telling you that a new phase is starting in your life. In that case the image is a sign of comfort and strength, so go ahead with confidence.

bed:

If it is your own bed, life may be good for you right now, especially as far as your love life is concerned. A strange bed could indicate unexpected academic success. Making a bed could suggest a change of some sort.

bee:

Bees have always been a sign of good fortune. But are you a busy bee or do you need to stop messing about and get your act together? Do you have a bee in your bonnet—do you keep going over a situation in your head? If you are stung, someone may let you down.

bell:

Ringing bells could mean news. What do the bells sound like? Are they urgent or joyful or alarming? Take note of the scenario in which the bells appear. It could be alerting you to an impending situation.

boat:

Any form of transport in the world of your imagination represents the progress you are making in life. Smooth journeys show that all is well; the opposite is true if it is stormy. Because water represents emotions, this symbol could be highlighting a relationship. If a storm is brewing, a challenge may lie ahead. If the boat sinks, maybe an idea has sunk and you need to change your plan. Are you drifting with the tide or just going with the flow in real life? Watching a boat sail away could suggest a lost opportunity.

boyfriend:

People can appear differently in your imagination than in real life, yet you know who they are. If this happens, your subconscious is telling you how similar these people are—they have common interests or looks that you like. Whether or not you have a boyfriend, this could suggest a need to feel loved and valued.

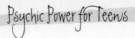

bruise:

This may be a warning from your inner guide that things are moving too fast. You need to slow down and calm down.

cake:

Food, provided it is of an enjoyable kind, generally denotes good health and happiness. If the food is stale, it could indicate the opposite—poor health, unhappiness, or a need to take better care of yourself.

candle:

Candles can be symbols of wisdom and understanding. Perhaps you are about to have a brilliant idea. If the candle goes out, there could be disappointment ahead. If it flickers, there could be a change in direction.

car:

A car usually represents your energy or drive. If something goes wrong with the car, it could mean that you are not using your talents properly or that you are out of control and need to put the brakes on. Running out of gas can suggest that you feel physically low. If the clutch won't work, your energy could be misdirected. If you have to push the car, perhaps you are pushing to get things done or need a bit of a shove to get moving. A crash could be a sign that you are totally out of control or are heading that way. Do take note of the road, because this is a sign of how your present path in life is looking. The condition and color and state of the car also give away lots of clues. Is it rusty? Have you let things slide a little? If it's sparkly, you are feeling great and ready to take on the next phase in your life.

carpet:

The message from your inner guide about the quality of your life right now will appear in the quality of the carpet. Is it beautiful and well cared for or is it threadbare and dirty?

castle:

Riches and opportunity are held in this symbol. It can also be a sign of security unless, of course, the castle is in ruins or if clouds surround the turret tops. If this is the case, are you building castles in the air?

cat:

Cats can represent intuition and instinct and are generally thought to convey help and luck, but much depends on how you feel about cats. A cat could remind you of someone you know who is catty, or it might represent your longing for independence and freedom.

chocolate or sweets:

Your inner guide may feel that you need a bit of pampering. Perhaps you have worked hard and now it is time to go out and treat yourself.

classroom:

A classroom could represent a part of you, and it can reflect what is happening to you right now and how you are feeling about it. You might be about to learn something important. Is there writing on the blackboard? What is the atmosphere in the room like? Are you in conflict with the teacher, or listening? Identify what is going on—it could be important.

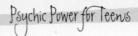

climbing:

This can represent ambition and a desire to succeed. The measure of your success is shown by how hard or how easy your climb is. For instance, if you are climbing a staircase, are the stairs firm or rickety? Is the mountain rocky or grassy? Is the ladder strong or flimsy? Do you feel secure? Do you reach the top? If you are climbing down, there could be unfinished business to deal with and a need to pay more attention to what is going on around you.

color:

Colors have their own special power and can communicate qualities that you might need to incorporate into your life. Do make sure that you take in the details of the color, because this also may send a message to you. Is it strong and bright, or dark and murky, or faint and barely noticeable? Remember, the following list only gives you suggestions—the way you interpret colors is unique to you. Listen to the gentle voice of your intuition and it will help you make sense of the color you experience.

black:

Black is often considered negative, but it is in fact a sign of movement and transition from one phase to another, or rest before the beginning of a new day. It is a color of quiet strength, protection, and groundedness.

blue:

This is the color of loyalty, truth, and justice as well as teamwork and harmony. It can also be a sign of being too deeply involved in things at the expense of others.

brown:

A down-to-earth and practical color. This is the color of devotion and loyalty, but it can also indicate being overly harsh or critical.

gold:

A symbol of success and achievement—and often wealth, too. A very rewarding phase in life.

green:

The color of honesty, healing, balance, peace, hope, and opportunity to start something new. Or perhaps the phrase "green with envy" comes to mind, or the phrase "green as grass," suggesting a need to grow up and take more responsibility for yourself.

orange:

A love of fun, creativity, and color. A rejuvenating color and a sign of confidence, telling you to believe in yourself and go for it.

pink:

There is simplicity in this color, suggesting peace and happiness.

red:

The color of power and strength and energy. Can also reflect strong emotions, such as passionate love or anger. Are you the passionate or angry one, or are you arousing passion or anger in others by your attitude and behavior? Or do you simply want to paint the town red?

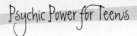

silver:

An idea will soon come to you, or a plan you are working on needs to be developed. Silver is the sign of the moon, and it could be suggesting that you need to pay more attention to your intuition. If you are too dreamy or romantic, perhaps it is time for you to see things more realistically.

violet and purple:

When these colors appear they convey intelligence and principles. Violet is the color of sensitivity and high ideals, so take its message to heart. Are you being oversensitive, or are you not sensitive enough? Purple is a wonderful color because it is transforming and puts everything into perspective.

white:

A fresh start, inspiration, purity, and protection. If you experience a shaft of light, it may mean that something or someone is being illuminated in your life. If there is no other color with the white, it could suggest loneliness or feelings of isolation.

yellow:

Yellow represents light, laughter, creativity, and intuition. Or do you associate this color with cowardice? If the yellow is wishy-washy, it may be a sign that your energy is low and you need a rest or health check.

computer:

This can indicate a need for more logic in a situation. Or do you need to work something out soon? Your inner guide is telling you that you can improve yourself and increase your understanding if you work at it.

crocodile:

What do you think about crocodiles in normal life? Do they scare you or do you admire them? They could be a warning to watch out for hypocrisy and lies—shedding crocodile tears! Or have you, or someone you know, been a bit snappy?

crying:

A healthy sign that suggests the release of tension and stress. Have you been upset? Is there a sense of loss in life? Or are you simply exhausted right now?

daffodil:

An early spring flower. Is love on your mind?

dagger:

Daggers, like swords and spears, are masculine symbols showing power, authority, determination, courage, and justice. Remember, anything that you hold is really an extension of yourself, and the circumstances in your life are the key factors in unraveling the message. How the dagger is used and who is using it is important. Is it for attack or defense? Is there someone who may stab you in the back, or do you need to find the power to go forward?

death:

Don't get upset by this symbol—it doesn't mean that someone is going to die. It simply indicates a major change, a transition from old to new. It really is a positive symbol, because with endings there are always new beginnings.

dieting:

Has food or losing weight been on your mind? Or do you need to cut back on some excess or distractions in your day-to-day life?

dog:

Dogs symbolize loyalty, friendship, protection, and trust to many people. Much depends, though, on how you feel about dogs. What characteristics do you associate with dogs? Does the dog remind you of anyone? What breed of dog is it? This can be significant. Guide dogs suggest a need to look where you are going, sheep dogs are for gathering and collecting, Alsatians are rescue dogs, and so on.

doll:

This could indicate happiness at home, or the need for greater harmony at home. Again, your inner guide will know which applies to you.

dolphin:

Symbols of guidance through troubled waters, healing, and well-being, the dolphin is also associated with playfulness. Do you need to lighten up about something?

door:

An open door is an opportunity. Are you ready to go through and enter the next phase in your life? A closed door may suggest that the time isn't right for a change and that you need to think of alternative ways to get what you want.

dove:

Very positive symbol of peace, hope, communication, love, and calmness. Is this what you need in your life right now? Or are you in the role of peacemaker?

drowning (also suffocating):

It's a sink-or-swim situation. Are you being swamped by your emotions, by exams, or by other commitments? Are there relationship troubles? Are you in too deep? Whatever the situation, this symbol suggests that you need to come up for air fast.

drunk:

Your inner guide could be warning you about something. Are you spending more than you can afford? Are all your friends to be trusted?

eagle:

Symbol of power, creation, success, and new horizons, but also of patience and waiting for the right moment to make your move. Do you need to use your eagle eye in a certain situation?

eating:

Is there something you need to chew over, or do you need to taste a new experience? Is there something you need to think

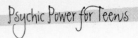

about—something that provides food for thought? Eating is generally a social event, so this symbol may mean that you need to be more cooperative.

electricity:
Surprises could lie ahead for you. Enjoy this exciting time in your life.

embarrassment:
Do you feel vulnerable or lacking in self-confidence? Do you feel that you're a bit of an outcast because you can't keep up with the crowd? The answer can't be found outside, in the material world of friends and school—the answer can only be found within. You need to believe in yourself more.

escaping:
This is all about taking responsibility and finding freedom. What are you escaping from? This symbol may represent your desire to control or release yourself from a certain situation. Do you need to face up to a decision? Perhaps you just have too much energy and need to let off steam.

exam:
Do you know the answers? Is the paper blank or do you see the answers? Have you forgotten your pen? Don't worry—this doesn't mean you are going to fail. These are simply classic example of anxieties in daily life coming to the surface.

eye:

Do you sometimes see the image of an eye floating toward you? If you do, is there something you need to focus on? What is the color of the eye you see? Any kind of injury or defect in the eye highlights a lack of clarity and focus in real life. Are you looking past the obvious?

falling:

A lack of confidence; a sense of insecurity or fear of failure. What situation in life is making you feel anxious? Do you feel you have a reputation to live up to, or are you just afraid of heights?

fame or famous people:

Do you long for more attention or recognition? This might also be a message urging you to work harder in order to realize your full potential.

family:

What are your relationships and attitudes toward family life like? Is it time to see someone or something in a new light?

fashion and clothes:

Are you worrying too much about what others think of you? Is it time to work on your self-image? What color are the clothes? Dark ones could suggest an attempt to hide. Bright ones suggest you may want to be noticed.

father figure:

How you get on with your father in real life affects how you understand what the symbol is releasing and reflecting.

Sometimes father figures, policemen, and teachers are all interchangeable, because essentially they all represent authority and power. Do you need to follow the rules? Do you need to seek advice, or do you need to follow your own rules?

fear:

Fear can be felt and revealed in many forms. Trust your inner guide to help you challenge negative thinking and find ways to overcome it.

fence:

Do you feel fenced in at the moment? Are you being stopped from doing something you want to do in waking life, or have you put up the barrier yourself? What is beyond the fence? Is it better or worse on the other side?

fighting:

Are you struggling with anger and frustration, or do you need to stick up for yourself or someone or something you care about?

fire:

The symbol of fire can represent your energy levels and enthusiasm for life. If the fire is warm and cozy, this can suggest contentment and security, but if the fire is wild then your inner emotions may be out of control. You'd better cool it. If you are in love, the fire could represent the passion of your feelings.

flowers and gardens:

Gardens and flowers are associated with peace, beauty, and harmony. But take a close look at the garden. Is it well cared for or overgrown? Are the flowers blooming or wilting? Are you using your talents or letting them go to waste? If you are walking down a garden path, note its condition and where it leads. If it is stony and unkempt, you may currently be experiencing problems.

fox:

Do you feel threatened by someone or something? Remember, facing fear is the best and only way to move beyond it.

ghost:

Have you been watching too many spooky movies? It could be time to clear away negative images and fear before they get buried in your subconscious and start to do real damage.

girlfriend:

As with boyfriends, this could suggest a need for friendship and acceptance from your peers. Jealousy could be playing itself out if you see your girlfriend with someone else.

grass:

As is the case with gardens and flowers, this symbol is fortunate if the grass is seen as green and flourishing.

grave:

Stop watching scary movies before you go to bed! This symbol doesn't have anything to do with death and dying—it is just a way for your inner guide to communicate information to you.

Nonetheless, this is still an important symbol, so note everything you can about the grave. Is there something grave or serious you need to think about? Perhaps the grave is a reflection of your loneliness, work overload, or the need to bury the past or end a relationship.

gun:

A warning that something could be about to happen in real life. Think of a starting gun, which is fired to begin a race. Are you holding the gun or is someone else holding it? Do you feel nervous about something but want to win too? Being shot at or having a gun pointed at you could indicate an enemy or feeling threatened.

hair:

Hair draws your attention to how you are feeling about yourself right now. What condition is your hair in? Combing hair and sorting out tangles shows your ability to solve problems. Having your hair cut suggests a new start, and washing your hair is all about washing out the old so you can emerge fresh and sparkling from top to toe.

hammer:

As long as the hammer is used for constructive purposes, this can be a good sign in every way. Progress is being made in all areas of your life.

hand:

A hand with the palm held up is a sign to stop. Clumsy hands or not being able to reach something could mean you can't hold on to situations in daily life or are losing your touch. Have you neglected work, a friend, or yourself? If the hands are injured or burned, perhaps you feel guilty or can't make a decision for fear of making a mistake.

home:

Home is often a symbol for your personality and your life. Every room represents a different aspect. Take a good long look inside the house. What is the atmosphere like? Is it bright, tidy, and fresh, or in need of a good cleaning? Are the rooms in the house empty? Do you feel lonely or empty in real life? If you go down to the basement, this can represent the secret hidden aspect of your life that is yet to be discovered. If you go upstairs, your fortunes could be about to change for the better. The condition on the outside of the house also gives important information about your image.

horoscope:

Generally a warning that you are being influenced too much by someone or something. Remember, developing your psychic power is all about taking control of your life, not letting others take control of it.

horse:

Horses are symbols of strength and wisdom, and they also represent swift thought and action. Sitting on a horse is positive; falling off of it is not so positive. If the horse is out of control,

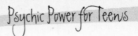

perhaps you are struggling with certain subjects at school. A gentle canter, on the other hand, shows that life is okay.

hospital:

Buildings are often symbols that represent ourselves. Because hospitals are places of healing, we tend to dream of them when we feel run down. Do you need to take better care of yourself and your health?

ice:

Your inner guide is warning you not to distance yourself too much from the love of family and friends. You do need their support, even if you don't think you do.

illness:

To experience images of illness can be a warning to take better care of your health. If you see someone else being ill, it could mean that you are worried about him or her. On a different level, the image may be telling you that your current plans are not healthy.

ink:

If the ink is spilled, there could be separation from old friends as you begin a new phase in your life, such as starting college or work. Your inner guide wants to reassure you that this is entirely natural and that you will make new friends.

insect:

Do you feel annoyed or irritated by petty issues in your life? Insects are often thought of as unpleasant and hostile and irritating. Dark moths suggest that someone is bugging you. Swarms of bees or wasps or ants could mean that you are anxious about something. Butterflies, though, are the exception—they can indicate a transformation in your life.

invisible:

Invisibility indicates a desire to disappear or to leave something or someone behind. Do you feel that there is no way out? Are you shy? Do you feel that you are too fat, too thin, or even worthless? If people disappear, the message is the same—a feeling of insignificance is being reflected and it is time to become more expressive in real life.

island:

Feelings of isolation are suggested by this—you either want to get away from it all or you want to be rescued. The water around the island represents emotional issues in your life. At the moment you are on safe ground, but you can't put your life on hold forever.

jewels and jewelry:

Good fortune and success are suggested by jewels, but much depends on what the jewels look like. Are they dull or bright and clear? On a deeper level jewels represent the hidden treasures of truth and understanding, so they can be an indication that you are making great progress with your psychic work.

journey:

Symbol of your journey through life. Are you starting the journey? Are you enjoying the journey? Are you lost? Are there obstacles ahead? Do you meet people? What are the colors of the landscape? There are countless clues here for you to think about.

juggler:

Are all the balls in the air, or do you miss catches? Are you coping, or do you need to take some time out to regroup and drop out of activities that are less important?

jungle:

A symbol of a new and exciting phase in your life. To avoid confusion and ensure success make sure that you are well prepared, alert to potential danger, and know where you are going and what you want to achieve.

key:

A key is a delightful symbol, because it suggests that you are opening to new possibilities. You could be about to find a solution to a problem. If you lose the key or can't find it, you are searching for a solution. Or is someone handing you the key to his or her heart? Sometimes your inner guide likes to play word games with you.

killing:

As a symbol it can mean that a phase is coming to an end and you need to start something new.

kiss:

Symbolic of a loving and affectionate situation. To be kissed can show approval, but to be kissed by someone you don't like suggests that you may have to do something you don't like. Also heed the warning about kiss and tell. Perhaps there is a lot of gossiping going on around you?

kitchen:

The house symbolizes you and your personality, and the kitchen is the center of the home. So this symbol reflects something or someone close to your heart. Is the kitchen a mess? Perhaps you feel confused or keep disagreeing with your parents. Is it tidy? Are things going well at home? Are you cooking? You could be involved in some creative project at present.

kite:

The interpretation of this symbol depends on the circumstances. If the kite flies easily, perhaps success is likely; the higher it goes, the better the sign.

knot:

A complication. Perhaps there is a complex situation in your life. Can you untie the knot and sort things out? If you make the knot bigger, are you making things worse? Are you tying up loose ends? Is it time to finish all those unfinished projects?

ladder:

A ladder is an important symbol because it relates to hopes and ambitions and your ability to move on to something new.

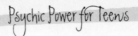

Are you going up in the world, or are you finding it hard going? If the ladder is missing rungs, perhaps you are nervous about something.

landscape:

This symbol depends on the circumstances. If the landscape is fine and gives you a good feeling, it is an indication of success and happiness. If the view is obscured by hills or forest, there could be some obstacles and troubles ahead.

leg:

If the legs are heavy, sore, or injured and you can't run, there could be difficulties in real life. There may be things you'd rather not do—for example, take an exam. Or perhaps you need to slow down and not be so impulsive.

letter:

Symbol of news that is heading your way.

library:

Symbol for learning and finding things out. Do you need to remember something important? Have you buried an aspect of yourself in the past? Are you searching for a book? Is there something you are looking for in real life? Of course, it could also mean that you just need to renew your overdue library books!

light:

Symbol of illumination and clarity after a period of confusion. You may get an answer or solution to a problem soon. If you see a light bulb, take note of the color. If light is flooding through an open door, something new is coming to you and things could get better soon.

lightning:

A flash of inspiration, although your inner guide warns you that dark clouds may accompany it. If you can persevere through the hard times you will be certain of success.

lion:

A symbol of strength, encouragement, and courage. Do you need to be strong, or is something in real life making you feel anxious? Lions can be scary too! Generally, though, a sign of encouragement and protection.

luggage:

A symbol that could suggest difficulties or burdens, though it depends on the quantity of the luggage you have and whether you could deal with it successfully.

makeup:

Are you hiding behind a mask because you are not happy with yourself or because you want to look your best? A clown-face makeup can suggest that you are putting on a brave face but feel unhappy underneath. Perhaps you need to find ways to boost your self-confidence and happiness in real life.

map:

Your inner guide is urging you to organize your time better and avoid distractions that are slowing you down.

marriage:

You could be about to strike up a new friendship or relation-ship or get together with someone to work on a project. Take note of all the details to find your message. What colors do you see? Who is getting married?

mask:

A symbol of treachery and deceit. Are you being entirely honest with yourself and others?

money:

Generally a symbol of good luck, recognition, or something good coming your way. Losing money could indicate losing something of value, like a friendship.

moon:

Symbol for women, intuition, and imagination. Think about your relationships with your mother or female friends. A new moon often means a new start. A full moon could suggest a time of great happiness. A moonlit scene suggests that all might not be well, and that you need to use your feelings and intuition more before making any decisions.

mother:

The mother symbol is nurturing and caring, whether you get along with your mother or not. Some good and helpful advice may be coming your way.

mountain:

Another symbol indicating obstacles to be overcome. There may be a lot of hard work, but your inner guide is urging you to climb to the top and achieve the success you deserve.

music:

In whatever way your inner guide experiences music, it brings the inspirational message that happiness and harmony are all around you if you just take the time to look.

needle or pin:

Perhaps there are disagreements with loved ones. Your inner guide is urging you to try to see things from another person's point of view. To be close to someone doesn't mean that you have to think and be alike. To be close to someone is to love and accept them for who and what they are, without trying to change them.

nudity:

This is all about embarrassment, fearing that you are going to make a fool of yourself in real life, or that others will laugh at you. Or it could be warning you that you are being too open and shouldn't lay yourself bare.

number:

There is an ancient magic and mystery behind numbers. Lots of people dream of seeing the lottery numbers. The trick is to remember them! To see your house number suggests an event involving home and family. To see telephone numbers means you may hear from someone soon. Numbers are symbolically

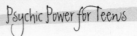

important, and each one carries a different meaning. The message from your inner guide will be found in whatever that number means:

one:

The number one can refer to you being number one. Do you need to establish your identity in real life? Perhaps you need to find your individuality and distinguish yourself from the crowd. Perhaps this number is encouraging you to stand up for yourself or for what you believe in. Perhaps it is encouraging you to become more independent. Alternatively it could be a new beginning or winning at something. It also could be the start of something new and the magic of new possibilities. On the other hand, it could be a warning against being selfish or pushy.

two:

The number two symbolizes relationships, both sexual and nonsexual. It's the sign of a twosome—girlfriend and boyfriend, or a close friendship between girls. It can also suggest the desire for a special relationship or the need for balance. Is there a relationship in your life that needs to be kept in balance with equal give and take? Are you giving too much or taking too much? The number two may also mean that you need to put yourself in someone else's shoes or see an alternative point of view before making any decisions.

three:

Three is the number of creativity, happiness, joy, and the need for expressing what is true in your heart. It refers to your talents, style, and self-expression. Three encourages you to develop your creativity. It is also the number of fun, so it could be a sign of good things coming your way. In fairy tales there are always three wishes. Perhaps it is time for you to make yours.

four:

Four is linked to practical matters, hard work, a need for order, self-discipline, and focus—a reminder that there is work for you to do or that you have duties to fulfill. If you feel positive about the number, it is telling you that you can achieve great things if you get organized and get on with your work.

five:

Five represents adventure. You should try something new or consider other options in your waking life. Perhaps it is time to be more alert, adventurous, sharp, and experimental. If this number appears, your mind is telling you to go on, explore, take a risk, give it a go—you have nothing to lose but your fear!

six:

Six is a number that represents harmony, wisdom, and knowledge. It is also the number of honesty and sincerity, so it could be pointing to someone who is sincere and genuine in your life. This person can be trusted with your secrets and can give you advice if you have a problem. Alternatively, the number six may be suggesting that there is a need for more honesty in your life. Perhaps you need to look for harmony

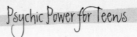

and balance in your life, or you may need to take better care of yourself.

seven:

The number seven is associated with music, art, and literature, and when it appears it could be an encouragement to develop your skills and talents in these fields. Alternatively, if in real life you tend to be a bit of a daydreamer, this number may be telling you to be more practical and down-to-earth. Perhaps you need to spend less time alone and more time with other people.

eight:

Just by writing down a figure eight you can feel its continuous flow. That means this number is telling you to relax a little and go with the flow. You could be in a lucky phase in which everything is going well. The number is often connected with material wealth and riches, so it could be a sign that good fortune is coming your way.

nine:

Nine is associated with caring, sharing, and giving. Perhaps you will either be helping someone out or someone will be helping you out. Nine is also the number of unselfishness, so if you see this number in your dreams you are probably a kind and thoughtful person. If you know that you are not, then the number is telling you to stop being so mean.

ten:

Ten is a symbol of wholeness, perfection, and completion. Have you worked hard and achieved a well-earned goal? Ten is the perfect number, and it marks the satisfactory ending of some chapter in your life. Now you can go to the next step or phase with greater understanding and confidence. It says that you are moving forward. Well done!

eleven:

The number eleven means that you are or soon will be feeling very inspired. It could also be telling you to pay more attention to your intuition—those illogical feelings you have when you do or say something and then either feel good or not quite right about it, and you can't explain why.

zero:

A zero means that you are full of energy and untapped potential. You just haven't found anywhere to direct it yet, so you need to find your inspiration. What makes your heart sing? Once you find the right place to channel your energy, nothing can keep you from achieving the success and recognition you deserve.

nurse:

Your inner guide is urging you to try a more caring approach to a difficult situation or person, or to take better care of yourself.

office:

A symbol of routine in daily life. What is the office like? If the office is a mess, maybe you need to get more organized. Looking through files means you may need to check up on someone or something. Seeing a photocopier might mean that you need to copy someone's good example.

orchard:
What season of year is it in your dream? Spring, a time of new beginnings; summer, a time of growth; autumn, a time of reflection; or winter, a time of endings? What is the condition of the fruit on the trees? Is it ripe and ready for the picking, suggesting that the opportunities you are hoping for are coming your way, or is it rotten and ready to fall?

oven:
Your inner guide is urging you to be careful and patient.

owl:
A symbol of wisdom, experience, and clarity of vision. It might be encouraging you to sharpen your wits. Let the owl's wisdom speak to you. It brings good advice.

oyster:
A symbol of happiness in love, if you are patient. For school and work it suggests that you can succeed if you work hard and show courage and determination.

package or present:
Good news or a nice surprise is on the way—depending of course on whether the contents are pleasant or unpleasant. Packing a box can be a symbol of getting rid of a bad habit. Your inner guide is encouraging you to clear away and prepare for a new start.

parents:

If you feel safe and secure, this image means your home life is good, but if you feel anxious this could reflect problems at home. Talk to your parents or get advice from a teacher you feel able to confide in.

party:

Partying represents your current enjoyment of life. Is the party great fun or is it a bit weird? If the latter, maybe you are finding it hard to relate to your friends at the moment.

pearl:

A very favorable symbol, but you will have to earn your success by hard work. Be patient and you will do well.

prison:

A symbol of isolation or feeling trapped in real life. Being unable to find the key suggests that you are trying to work things out in real life but can't put your finger on a solution. If you find the key, you'll find the answer to your problems.

prize:

A symbol of achievement in real life. Your inner guide is just giving you a pat on the back and saying "well done."

quicksand:

Do you feel that you are sinking deeper and deeper and you can't escape? Do you feel insecure or helpless? Is it time to pull out before it is too late?

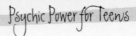

race:

Are you lagging behind or are you winning? Races usually symbolize the progress we are making in life. Perhaps you need to be more competitive in real life, especially if you are a bit laid-back. If you are winning the race, it shows that you feel on top of things.

rain:

A symbol of cleansing and washing away fear, stress and anxiety. After the storm a period of calm and happiness will follow.

rainbow:

A great symbol that holds the magic of true promise. The storm has passed and good times lie ahead. Take note of the colors of the rainbow, and look at the "color" section of this glossary to analyze this symbol more deeply.

rash:

Could be a warning against speaking before you have a chance to think. Try to think carefully about the results of your words.

rat:

A warning symbol. Who is behaving like a dirty rat? Who is letting you down? Have you gotten in with the wrong crowd?

restroom:

You could be feeling vulnerable at the moment and may have a fear of being found out. Restrooms are places where you clean up and get rid of things, so the symbol could be hinting that it's time for you to clear up the clutter in your life. This could range from tidying your room to getting rid of bad habits or stressful relationships.

riding:

Riding a horse is a fortunate sign, unless the horse is out of control or throws you.

river:

A river is a symbol of how the course of your life is flowing right now, particularly regarding your feelings, because water symbolizes emotions. Is the water muddy or clear, fast moving or running smoothly? If there are boulders or a waterfall, there may be disagreements. If you are struggling upstream, there may be difficulties with family or friends. If you are getting out of your depth, things could be going wrong in your real life.

rotten:

Anything rotten is a symbol of decay, which will affect you deeply. Your inner guide is urging you to take better care of your health.

sand:

Many small irritations could be holding you back. Try not to let them get you down, and keep your eye on the bigger picture.

school:

A sign that there is something you need to learn, and life is about to teach you that lesson. It could also be drawing your

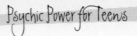

attention to the importance of your schoolwork or an incident that happened at school.

scissors:

Scissors generally mean cutting out or giving up something in waking life. Do you need to cut loose from a bad habit or a situation? If the scissors seem threatening, could it be that someone is jealous of you?

sex:

A natural and healthy sign for mind, body, and spirit. If you imagine yourself as a boy when you are a girl and vice versa, this doesn't mean you need a sex change! It is your inner guide telling you to pay more attention to either the masculine qualities of assertiveness or the feminine qualities of nurturing or caring.

shoe:

The condition of the shoe is a big clue to how you feel about yourself in real life. If the shoes are scruffy and worn, perhaps you feel tired or fed up, or things are getting you down. If they are bright and shiny, you feel optimistic about life and things are going well. If you can't find your shoes, perhaps you need to stop wasting time and get down to what is important.

smell:

To experience a beautiful fragrance means happiness and success. But take heed if the smell is unpleasant. Something fishy is going on. It's the same with taste. Pleasant tastes are a good sign. Unpleasant ones suggest caution.

smiling:

This is one of the best symbols, whether you are smiling or you see someone else smiling. This symbol means that all is well in your world right now.

snake:

A symbol of the creative male force. However, if the snake is coiled, it represents the feminine. Snakes also represent sexual desire. Have you got the hots for someone? Also see the "animal" section of this glossary for other interpretations.

spider:

A spider often symbolizes good fortune, but if in real life you are scared of them, it could mean that some of your friends don't have your best interests at heart.

stamp:

These can be any type of stamps—postage stamps, rubber stamps, etc. Perhaps your inner guide is urging you to listen to the voice of authority, be it from parents or teachers.

sun:

Ancient symbol of masculine energy, just as the moon symbolizes feminine energy. A symbol of light, life, and power, the sun is a good sign. Your inner guide is telling you that you can't fail—you are a winner.

sword:

Your inner guide could be urging you to make a decision of some sort.

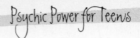

taste:

See "smells"

teeth:

Beautiful white teeth suggest health and happiness, while rotten or missing teeth suggest rough times ahead, or feelings of rejection. On a simpler level, you may just need to visit the dentist!

telephone:

News is on the way. If you can't hear what is being said, your inner guide is urging you to listen more to what others are saying in real life. If you can't get in touch with someone, you may feel that people aren't listening to you. Perhaps you need to find a sympathetic friend. It could even be your mom or dad!

theater:

Are you watching or taking part? This is a symbol of the theater of life. Take note of what is being played out on the stage. Being on a stage is all about recognition, so maybe in real life you are longing to be noticed. This image is suggesting that with a little more confidence you could really shine.

thinness:

Seeing yourself as thin could be a sign that you are stretching yourself too thin or a sign that you are too concerned about appearance. Your inner guide is urging you to think less about how you look and more about how you feel about yourself.

tiger:

A symbol of power, strength, and depth of vision. This symbol is connecting you to these characteristics and reinforcing your own abilities. Seeing a tiger's face suggests that you need to be more watchful in real life. Tigers are dynamic and full of energy, so be encouraged by this symbol to go for the gold in your real life.

train:

A symbol of your journey through life and the present phase you are in. Are you getting onto a train? This could be the start of a new phase. Are you sitting? Do you feel relaxed and comfortable with life? Are you feeling jostled by overcrowding? This could mean you feel under pressure.

tree:

An ancient symbol of strength and protection and the life force within you. A tree that is bare of leaves is a reminder to conserve your energy but to keep working consistently and quietly. If your tree is dead, this could suggest you feel low in spirits and need a rest. To see a tree in full leaf suggests good health and creativity.

triangle:

A symbol of choice. You may need to choose between two boyfriends or girlfriends or make a decision about school or work.

tunnel:

If you can't find your way out, you could be going through a confusing and scary time in real life. Is there a light at the end of

the tunnel? If a train is coming at you, you could be on a collision course with someone or something in real life.

umbrella:

Because water represents feelings, an umbrella shows that you have the power to rise above whatever may happen in real life, and you will be shielded from harm. Your inner guide is reassuring you that you can cope with whatever challenges lie ahead. If your umbrella is damaged in some way, this could suggest vulnerability.

umpire:

Arguments are indicated. Your inner guide is urging you to find a solution that works for everyone, not just for you.

uniform:

A symbol of rules and authority. Do you find it hard to conform, or do you have no problems obeying rules and regulations? How do uniforms make you feel?

university:

A symbol of learning, so perhaps you need to find out more facts before you press ahead with your plans.

valentine:

You have more admirers than you realize, but all this counts for nothing if you don't admire yourself. Your inner guide is urging you to build your self-esteem.

vampire:

Because legend says that vampires thrive by sucking people's blood, this symbol means that you should ask yourself who in your real life may be draining your energy. Is someone demanding your attention, or are you too demanding of yourself and doing far too much?

vegetable:

A symbol of good health, depending, of course, on what state the vegetables are in. If they are ripe and delicious, you are brimming with health and vitality. Rotting vegetables may mean that you are wasting your potential with poor eating habits and lack of exercise.

volcano:

The key word here is "erupting," so perhaps you need to blow your top about something. On the other hand, it could be a warning that you or someone you know needs to cool down.

vulture:

Watch out for people who may not be what they seem. This could also suggest that instead of doing your own work you are relying too much on other people. Have more confidence in yourself.

walking:

A symbol of measured and steady movement toward your goals in life. Other forms of movement—car, train, cycling, and so on—have a similar meaning. All of these comment on the progress you are making in waking life. In your dream, do you encounter difficulties when you walk? This could be a warning that challenges are coming up in real life. Are you ambling along? This could be a warning from your inner guide that you need to stop wasting time. If, on the other hand, you stop to enjoy the walk or take time to look at the flowers, it means that you are enjoying your life at the moment.

wall:

Symbol of an obstacle or boundary that is presenting a challenge to you. Do you find your way around the wall, or do you climb over it?

war:

A symbol of anxiety, tensions, and stress. Trust your inner guide to help you find ways to face and overcome your fears.

water:

Water symbolizes emotions, and it is the form and condition of the water that gives the clues here. For example, huge ocean waves may imply that you are overwhelmed by your feelings. If the water is muddy and murky, you may feel confused about things. Washing yourself could be a sign that you need to clean up your act. If you wash your hands, you may want to have nothing to do with someone or something. If you are drowning, things are seriously getting the best of you. If the water is stagnant, then your inner guide is telling you that you need to develop new interests and new friends. But to gaze over a calm lake or swim in a warm, blue sea is a positive message that life is fine, your emotions are well-balanced, and you are feeling happy and at ease.

window:

A comment on your current view of life. If there are curtains in the way or the windows are dirty, you may not be seeing clearly at present. If you see a beautiful landscape, this suggests that the future looks promising. If the scenery is ragged, there could be problems ahead, perhaps disagreements with friends. A brick wall suggests frustration, and a mountain indicates lots of hard work.

wizard and witch:

A symbol of magic entering your life. This could be your psychic work, or it could be the start of a new relationship.

wolf:

A positive symbol that shows protection, caring, and healing. On the other hand, it could be a warning of deception—as in the saying "wolf in sheep's clothing." Perhaps you need to watch out for someone you know who is not all they seem.

young people or children:

A symbol of newness and freshness. Your inner guide is telling you it's time to start a new chapter in your life.

zoo:

Cages are often a sign of feeling trapped in real life. On the other hand, a zoo could also suggest meeting new friends and possibly traveling to exotic countries. What animals are in the zoo? What characteristics and similarities remind you of yourself or people you know in real life?

Index